To Greg Jr. for being so patient and so filled with grace

To Connie and Matt, who have been so supportive
of our journey

To Ed Dobson, who departed prematurely and whose
wisdom and counsel put us on a trajectory to bring
healing and restoration to our family

Contents

Contents

Embracing
the Journey

Authors' Note

Throughout this book, we use the phrase LGBTQ to refer to the broad community of people who are lesbian, gay, bisexual, transgender, queer, and/or questioning—essentially, all those whose sexual orientation or gender identity falls outside the majority experience.

Foreword

Dear Mom and Dad,

Thank you. My entire life you have stressed the importance of good manners and social etiquette with me. When I was little, you taught me to say "please" when I asked for something and "thank you" once I had received it. Now that I am a fully grown adult, I realize that I haven't always used my manners when communicating with you. Please allow me to properly thank you for everything you have done for me, and everything I know you will continue to do.

Thank you for sharing our family's story with others.

Thank you for your honesty.

Thank you for building bridges between the LGBTQ community, their families, and God.

Thank you for your boldness to speak out against the things that you refuse to accept.

Thank you for your bravery.

Thank you for making me stubborn. If I wasn't stubborn, I doubt that your ministry or this book would have ever happened.

Thank you for not letting my abrasive words discourage you.

Thank you for being patient with me.

Thank you for loving me in spite of my numerous faults.

Thank you for loving me and my sister equally.

Thank you for not giving up on having a relationship with me.

Thank you for not kicking me out of the house once you learned that I was gay.

Thank you for removing fear from the equation within our relationship.

Thank you for not trying to change me.

Thank you for not sending me to gay conversion therapy.

Thank you for no longer attempting to "pray the gay away."

Thank you for accepting me as I am.

Thank you for never treating me like I am an embarrassment to you or our family.

Thank you for teaching me how to treat others with respect.

Thank you for demonstrating your compassion for others every day.

Thank you for giving me an empathetic heart.

Thank you for going to places and meeting people who are different from you.

Thank you for being slow to judge and quick to listen.

Thank you for reflecting your faith in a positive light with my friends.

Thank you for acting as surrogate parents to my LGBTQ friends, who years later still refer to you as McMom and McDad.

Thank you for continuing to be McMom and McDad for people in or connected to the LGBTQ community whom I have never met.

Thank you for welcoming the people I love into our family.

Thank you for putting me in contact with all the pastors and counselors who reassured me that it was okay that I am gay and a Christian.

Thank you for encouraging me to use the gifts that God has given me.

Thank you for always being my biggest cheerleaders.

Thank you for giving me the opportunity to be a part of your ministry.

Thank you for praying for me.

Thank you for encouraging my spiritual growth.

Thank you for continuing to love and support me.

Thank you for making me the man I am today.

I pray that God will use your story to mend broken relationships.

I pray that God will bless you for your efforts to help heal other hurting families.

I pray that God will protect you from people who may be angered by your ministry and your story.

I pray that God will soften their hearts and open their minds.

I pray that God will shield you from any misguided hatred.

I pray that God will not let you become discouraged.

I thank God that you are fighting the good fight.

I thank God that our relationship has been reconciled.

I thank God that you are my parents.

Love,
Greg McDonald Jr.

Preface

Embracing the Journey

For most of our lives, we lived near Lake Michigan. We both grew up playing in the water, and when we had our own family, we spent countless weekends and summer breaks in Harbor Springs, a quaint, Norman Rockwell–like community tucked along the lake's northeast shore. As Gordon Lightfoot says, Lake Michigan's "islands and bays are for sportsmen," and so we kept a boat there and spent hours on the crystal-clear water.

We quickly learned the importance of having a nautical chart or map any time we were on an unfamiliar part of the lake. If we found ourselves in new territory without anything to guide us, we had to stay on constant alert, standing on the bow of the boat and watching for hazards or currents that might take us somewhere we didn't want to go. After a few tense experiences like that, literally sailing blindly through the fog, we learned the value of being prepared. There were plenty of times when a depth chart warned us about an underwater obstacle that was invisible to the naked eye, or a map guided us to safety when a storm blew in and visibility disappeared.

It should be no surprise, then, that when we found out our son was gay, one of the first things we did was go to a bookstore, looking for some kind of map to guide us. (This was back in 2001, before the internet brought bookstores to our fingertips.) We'd been Christians for almost twenty years by that point, and so we first went to every Christian bookstore in Grand Rapids. When that didn't work, we went to the biggest bookstore in town. We wanted—no, we needed—some kind of help to navigate a situation like ours in a Christlike, Bible-honoring, church-serving way.

You know what we found? Nothing. The books about homosexuality back then all seemed to be written with some kind of political agenda, either from the left or the right. There was nothing personal about how to live as a family. There wasn't a single book available to help us understand how to navigate the turbulent and uncharted waters we found ourselves in as the Christian parents of a gay son.

We asked our pastor if he could introduce us to a family that was walking a similar path. Perhaps they could warn us about potential obstacles in the fog. You know what he told us? In a church of five thousand people, the pastor only knew of one family with a gay child, and he didn't think they would be willing to talk.

That's pretty much how it was for the next decade. We felt like we were on our own. The loudest voices in the American evangelical church community—a place where we otherwise felt accepted and loved, and where we grew personally and spiritually—were waging war against what they called the "gay agenda." Their messages often ignored families like ours, the frontline soldiers in their pews. Even talking about our situation made a lot of our closest Christian friends uncomfortable. Meanwhile, the gay community, understandably feeling attacked, alienated themselves from any conversation about God, let alone any genuine relationship with his followers; for many of them, all Bible believers were hypocrites and bigots.

There we were, in the middle of a storm without a map to help us to love our son, love God, and love the church all at the same time. We had no guidance for how to reconcile a lifetime of messages about the dangers of homosexuality with the reality of the person right in front of us. And, as Greg Jr. likes to remind us, we made plenty of mistakes. If there was something that we could do wrong, we probably did it.

But slowly, with a lot of hard work and God's grace, things started to change. *We* started to change. Our relationship with our son started to change. Today, the storms have quieted, and the sun has come out. To our surprise, we realized that we had charted a map of sorts for those who found themselves in these waters after us.

It started with an occasional phone call from a friend of a friend whose child had come out. They needed someone to help them process how to respond. It grew to mentoring dozens of parents one-on-one, and then facilitating small groups in our home, and then speaking to church groups and conventions across the country. We eventually started a ministry called Embracing the Journey, and we now share our story with thousands of people, from evangelical church leaders to gay teenagers, to help them better understand families like ours and embrace the "entire body of believers."

When we were just getting started, long before the outline of a future ministry started to take shape, a good friend asked us, "Are you ready to be the face of this?" In other words, are you willing to put yourself on the firing line between the church and the LGBTQ communities? To potentially be attacked on one side for not being open enough, and on the other for not being conservative enough?

The question made us pause. Were we ready? We're far from perfect role models. There are plenty of questions we still can't answer. Are we really the best spokespeople for how a family can grow and embrace their own journey?

But the counter question seemed stronger: if it wasn't us, then who would it be? God had led us through a series of experiences that put us in a unique place of understanding. How could we not use our journey to help others?

Because if we know one thing, it is that this is a journey. Our relationships with family, with friends, and even with God grow and change over time. We aren't the same people we were thirty-five years ago when we first became parents, and we're not the same people we were eighteen years ago, when we found out our son was gay. To get where we are today, we needed to go through all of the places, and emotions, in between. Eighteen years ago there was nothing about parenting a gay son that we wanted to "embrace." But now that's our whole ministry. We've learned to love the life God gave us, and we're now called to help others do so as well.

We've sat with mothers and fathers who approach this unexpected (and, let's be honest, often undesired) change in their family's life with grace and peace, and with others who feel their emotions boil over into anger, betrayal, or pain. We've sat with couples as they work through how to parent LGBTQ children transitioning, marrying, and having children, as well as suffering alienation, breakups, illness, and hate crimes. We know parents who turned their backs on their children, or on their church, or on God himself. We've also seen plenty of families who grew closer to one another and to God.

Yes, parenting is a journey, and being the Christian parent of a son or daughter who is LGBTQ is a very specific kind of journey. But it's one that, finally, doesn't have to be undertaken alone.

Most people, in our experience, navigate a three-part pattern as they move through unsought and unexpected events of life, including the discovery that your child is different than you expected.

First, we fear, then we survive, and finally we are ready to thrive.

Here's what we mean: As parents, we want the best possible life for our child—a life full of safety, security, and healthy relationships. As Christian parents, we pray that our child will build a strong, eternal relationship with God. But when a son or daughter comes out as lesbian, gay, bisexual, transgender, or queer/questioning, many of those pictures we've imagined disintegrate into dust. The dreams we once held for our child's future may seem shattered. Most of us first react, on some level, out of fear. There's a feeling of free-falling. This is all new, foreign territory, full of threats we've probably never considered. Did we do something wrong to make our child like this? Did God do something to make our child like this? Can they live a spiritually and emotionally fulfilling life this way? How will others treat them? How will others treat us? What will it do to our son or daughter's spiritual life? Are they abandoning us? Are they abandoning God? Are we abandoning God if we support our child?

As you'll see in the chapters that follow, we asked all these questions and a lot more. For us, at first, God didn't make sense. Our child didn't make sense. We found ourselves isolated, alone with a secret and alienated from a child we loved while he sorted through his own questions and decisions. It was a season of high emotions that revolved around a "high-voltage" topic, and it came with more questions than answers.

To be honest, in that painful early season, we had no desire to go on the journey God laid out for us. And we're not alone. Many parents confide that, in the initial shock of their life change, it feels like this is all a great big mistake, a cosmic accident that gave them a damaged child. The anger, and the temptation to lash out and say or do painful things, is strongest for most of us in those early years.

Yet panic only lasts for so long. Eventually our family moved to a kind of place where we could survive long term. It was uncomfortable to accept, but this was our family's new normal, and it was full of decisions about how we would live. Would we tell our friends? Would our church support us? Would our church support our son?

For Christian parents, the tension between their faith

and their child's identity may be strongest here. Many families we know lost friends, and sometimes their whole church community, when they chose to accept their child's identity. Others distanced themselves from their children, physically or emotionally or both. If parents maintain a connection with their LGBTQ son or daughter at all, conversations at first can become either tense or shallow. As we'll show you, there were long years with Greg Jr. where we were either arguing or retreating to just the "news, sports, and weather."

As children age and become adults themselves, the survival of the relationship shifts with them. Parents who are in this uncomfortable place often face a steady stream of individual choices: How do you handle the choices that come with an adult child living independently? How do you handle their relationships? The potential of their eventual marriage? What happens if they have children of their own?

We didn't recognize it at the time, but those years of survival were teaching us how to relate to Greg Jr. as an adult, and often it was only our son's patience and willingness to let us stumble that saved our relationship. We loved our son, but we also felt like it was our job to "fix" his spiritual life and to bring him—willing or not—back to what we had decided was God's plan for him.

Finally, with much prayer and through God's grace, our family's journey ended in a place where we graduated from fear, and from surviving, and we learned to embrace our journey, our life, and the family that God has given us. Without giving up God, or the church, or our faith, we learned to thrive in this new territory.

There were several things that helped us break through from a place of survival to the place where we are now, and we'll share those in the chapters that follow. Mostly, we'll focus on telling you the unvarnished truth of our own story, because we believe that people learn best through seeing examples. But at the end of each chapter, we'll also provide a summary for parents of "What We Learned," drawing out key learnings and principles that may help you in your own lives.

We understand that every situation, and every family, is unique. But when you're in the middle of uncharted and choppy waters, having the support of someone who's navigated the area before can be lifesaving. So, if you're curious how a Christian parent and an LGBTQ child can build a healthy relationship, this is how we found our way through. This is what happened when two middle-aged, white, evangelical Christians decided to open our doors, and then our hearts, to the LGBTQ community.

Today, we understand that God uniquely designed us to be Greg Jr.'s parents, just as much as he designed us for our daughter, Connie. We're experiencing a deeper, richer, more authentic relationship with Christ and with the people who he's put in our path. We have a relationship of love and respect with our son, now an adult, and lasting friendships with the people who Christ brought into our path because of Greg Jr. We have found our purpose in life through this journey.

What follows is our experience learning how to love our son, and love God, and love our church, even when those three seemed to be at odds with one another. We hope that it offers you hope for reconciliation and flourishing in your own faith and family, whatever that may look like.

This is the book we were hoping to find in that bookstore back in 2001, and the guide that hundreds of parents tell us they're desperate for today.

Take from it what you will. We're going to be honest about our mistakes, and also about the ways God has built something beautiful despite them.

Parenting is a journey to be embraced, whether your child is gay or straight, tall or short, athletic or clumsy. None of this has caught God by surprise. This is the child God chose specifically for us. And he did so for a reason.

We prayed for God to change our son. Instead, he changed us.

We're grateful every day that we have the privilege of being Greg Jr.'s parents.

Part 1

FEAR

"Are You?"

Greg

IT WAS A SUNNY Saturday in 2001, and the summer sun warmed the air around our home beside the Thornapple River in beautiful western Michigan. Lynn and I were getting ready to leave for the farmers' market in downtown Grand Rapids, one of our favorite things to do on the weekends.

But something kept bothering me. As Lynn gathered our shopping baskets for the market, I asked her to wait for me for a minute. "I want to check something," I said vaguely as I jogged down the stairs to Greg Jr.'s bedroom.

A few weeks before, I had been at lunch with my good friend Dan, who was a pastor. We met every Friday for years in an accountability relationship. Dan had recently confided that he'd found his teenage son, who was about the same age as Greg Jr., looking at porn on the internet. The thought had been nagging at me ever since.

"Surfing the web" was still a relatively new idea back then.

But I kept thinking about the desktop computer Greg Jr. had in his room, which we'd bought so that he could do schoolwork. Was he using it for anything else? This was the best chance I'd have to check it out. Greg Jr. was at work as a server at a local restaurant, and Lynn was distracted. I didn't want to worry her if I didn't have to.

I sat down at my son's desk and found that the computer was already on. Dan had explained to me how to check a browser's history to see what websites my son visited, and there it was.

The idea of my seventeen-year-old son looking at porn didn't shock me. I'd been looking at porn myself since I was about eight years old, when I'd snuck up behind my dad's recliner one night and discovered that he had a *Playboy* tucked inside the oversized *Life* magazine he was pretending to read. Once I knew what I was looking for, it wasn't hard to find his whole stash of magazines. I shared them with my friends, and then when I was old enough, I bought my own. Thirty years later, it was a temptation that still followed me.

But this website wasn't the kind of porn I was used to. There were two men on the screen, and no women.

A vise closed around my heart. My son—my only son, whom I was crazy about—was looking at gay porn. And he was doing it a lot, based on what I could see in the history.

Slowly, reluctantly, I called for Lynn. I think she could see it on my face before I said the words.

"Greg's been looking at porn."

Lynn

IN THAT SECOND, AS I looked at my husband's pain-filled expression, all I could think was *Let it be women. Don't let it be one of those websites.*

Yes, my first thought on hearing that my son was looking at porn was a hope that it would be "just" heterosexual porn. Which tells you, I guess, that the news that our son was gay wasn't a total surprise. But we'll talk about that more later.

Greg stepped away from the computer, and I saw the screen. Those weren't women.

I knew what I was looking at, but I still tried to deny it. "Maybe it was an accident," I started, turning to my husband with tears already forming in my eyes, begging him to give me a way out. "Maybe it was one of Greg Jr.'s friends who came over and used the computer."

Please, Jesus, let it be someone else's kid.

Greg didn't answer me, but from his expression I knew that wasn't it.

"Maybe . . ." But I had already run out of maybes.

My sweet, sensitive, tenderhearted boy—my artist, always surrounded by gorgeous girls but never dating them— had been hiding something from us. Something I'd been told could cost him his soul.

The tears were falling heavy now. "What are we going to do?" I whispered.

WE HAD STUMBLED INTO one of the most pivotal moments of parenting that we would ever have—the kind that can define, or break, a parent-child relationship for years to come.

Every parent has dreams for their child. We stare into infant eyes and try to imagine this little human as an adult. We picture sports games and first dates and graduations and weddings and grandchildren. But things rarely play out just as we imagine, do they? There are calls from the principal. Medical diagnoses. Failed tests and tryouts. Personality conflicts. A grandchild is born before a wedding. A graduation never happens. Sometimes a child's dreams or desires carry them far from home, either physically or spiritually.

Between 3 percent and 20 percent of parents in the United States (depending on which surveys you believe) will, like us, need to adjust to the idea that the person our child dreams of dating or marrying is probably not the gender we imagined for them back when they were babies. And at least another 1 percent of parents will learn that their child experiences gender dysphoria, which means that when they look in a mirror, the gender of the person they see doesn't match the gender they feel they are emotionally and psychologically.

Those are pretty big dreams to readjust.

Christianity and Western culture put a lot of importance on a person's gender and sexuality. The first words we hear when a child is born are "It's a boy" or "It's a girl," and from that moment, certain expectations are set. So even for liberal, progressive parents, discovering that "my child is gay" or "my child is transgender" can feel at first like someone pulled the rug out from under them, because it pushes them to see their child through a lens they didn't have before. And for those of us who live in traditional families, attend traditional churches, and surround ourselves with traditional family values, finding out that our child is gay or transgender can feel like a major earthquake.

Lynn

WHEN WE TALK ABOUT that moment, the one when we go from *not knowing* to *knowing,* many of the parents we meet say something like, "In an instant, my child—the person I'd known their whole life—seemed like a stranger to me."

When our understanding of a person shifts in a radical way, it's easy to start to think that our child isn't *anything* like we imagined they would be. We forget about the books or movies they love, or the way they play with their younger siblings, or the inside jokes we share at the dinner table. All we see is this big, flashing sign that says that they're *different.*

For many parents, especially those who didn't suspect anything was different until The Moment, it feels at first like a betrayal. We've been living for years with one family, and now someone—our child? Society? *God?*—just pulled a nasty switch on us and gave us someone else.

It's hard to adjust to a surprise like that.

I WAS TORN. ON one hand, I wanted to wait until Greg Jr. returned from work and demand that he explain himself, right then. I was itching for a confrontation and to bring this into the open.

On the other hand, I knew enough about parenting by then to understand that doing that could destroy our relationship beyond repair.

My tendency, like that of many parents, is to focus on myself when I get upset. Thank God that by this time in my life I'd learned the hard way what happened when my temper did the talking.

When all of the raging feelings fill us, too often we react first and think later. We want to express our anger toward the person who caused it. We want that person to know that they've done wrong. We want to take all our negative feelings and dump them on someone else, even if that person is a family member we love like crazy.

Looking for that kind of release is a natural human temptation, but when we act in the heat of the moment, it's easy to say things that we haven't thought through and things we don't really mean. And those things can cause serious damage.

Lynn and I know dozens of LGBTQ adults and their parents who still bear scars, years later, from painful words shared in the heat of the moment.

How could you do this to me?

I'm embarrassed by you.

I can't look at you.

I raised you better than this.

I wish you'd never been born.

Yes, parents say these things and so much worse.

That Saturday afternoon, seeing the porn on my son's computer, I was definitely tempted to confront Greg Jr. right away. But my relationship with my son was one of the most important things in my life, and Lynn and I both immediately understood that this conversation would be the single biggest thing that had ever happened to him and would set the tone between us for years to come.

We needed to approach this carefully in order to protect the relationship. But instead of confronting Greg Jr. when he came home, we did what we often did when we struggled for the answers to life's questions: we called our pastor.

For eleven years, Lynn and I had been members of Calvary Church in Grand Rapids, an evangelical congregation led by a phenomenal teacher named Ed Dobson. Over the years, we'd become friends with Ed and his wife, Lorna, and often turned to them for guidance on both spiritual and practical matters. We trusted him totally—not because of his title, but because of how well we knew his heart and the patient, steady love he showed everyone in his congregation.

Lynn

AS MUCH AS OUR world felt rocked, we knew that Saturday was one of Ed's days off, and Sunday was his busy day, full of services and committee meetings. Not wanting to interrupt him, we agreed to wait.

That weekend was excruciating. I basically went to bed, curled up in the fetal position, and stayed there. I could hear Greg trying to act casual when he ran into our son in the kitchen. "Mom's not feeling well" was all he said. Greg Jr., who was a teenager and also used to some tension in the house, just shrugged. If he sensed that the shift in mood was about him, he never let on.

First thing Monday morning, we called Ed's office, and something about the tone in Greg's voice must have told his secretary how important this was. Ed made time for us right away. As we drove toward the church, my mind fixed on a single question.

How could I choose between loving my child or loving God?

Because if Greg Jr. was gay, I was convinced I would have to give one of them up.

For years I'd heard the preachers on the radio and on TV talking about the "abomination" of homosexuality, and the dangers of the "gay lifestyle." I'd read the verse in 1 Corinthians that said that believers should "not associate with anyone who bears the name of brother if he is guilty of sexual immorality." Our family lived in a very homogeneous, very conservative community. Most Christians I knew would never, *ever* be friends with someone who was gay. That, to them—and to me, at the time—was a sin too horrible, a lifestyle too foreign to be endured.

But this wasn't a friend. This was my son.

As I lay in bed that weekend, I kept praying, over and

over, "Let this be a dream. Don't make us do this. We can't do this alone. My son needs help. We need help."

Would God really ask me to give him up?

Never to share a meal with him, hug him, wish him happy birthday, or have any influence in his life?

When we arrived at Ed's office, I was gasping for air, crying so hard I could hardly talk.

Greg

LYNN WAS A MESS. The pain in my own heart made it hard to take a breath, and I struggled with my words. Ed greeted us in the office lobby and silently offered us big, generous hugs. I couldn't remember the last time I'd felt so broken and lost.

Ed wasn't a very tall man; I think he was about five feet four inches. I'd recently teased him about whether he needed a boost to get into my Ford Expedition. That morning in his office I remember thinking that he looked particularly tiny as he sat there behind his desk, like a kid who needed a booster seat to be tall enough to reach the table. But behind his small stature was a giant heart and one of the most grounded people we knew.

I wish that every parent in our position could have a pastor like Ed. He knew and loved Greg Jr. He knew and loved us. And he knew Jesus better than anyone I'd ever met. As I told him our story and what we'd found, his eyes never wavered. He never winced.

"We need to know how to handle this," I finally told him.

"If our son really is gay, we need to know what a Christlike response looks like."

This phrase—"a Christlike response"—started with something simple; those were the days when a lot of people had "WWJD" bracelets and accessories, and "What would Jesus do?" was a question we heard a lot in church. In the years leading up to this meeting with Ed, I'd been more intentional about trying to bring that question off the bracelet on my wrist and into my everyday decisions at work and at home. Looking back now, I believe God pointed me that way on purpose, so that when I was faced with something so far above my spiritual pay grade, I at least knew where to start looking for answers.

Ed thought for a minute, choosing his words carefully. "I don't have the perfect answer for you. But I can tell you three things. First, Greg is your son, and your most important job right now is to love him. Don't turn away from him."

I could feel Lynn exhaling that part of her breath she'd been holding for three days. This had been her deepest fear.

"Second," Ed continued. "Be sure to love his friends. The gay community has been terribly mistreated, and in some ways, they have become the lepers of our society today. They are very good at circling around and supporting one another when they are hurting."

At the time I didn't understand how insightful this observation was, or how valuable it would become. But Ed wasn't done.

"Third," he said as he looked at us deeply, and with compassion that filled me. "It is normal to want to look in the mirror and try to see what each of your roles might be in your son's situation. But do not spend a lot of time there. Nothing positive will come from that."

That wasn't what I expected a Christian pastor to say, but his words touched me. There was so much compassion in Ed's voice that I found the first glimmer of hope.

"And there's another thing," Ed continued, his soft Irish brogue still audible after more than twenty years in this country. "Trust that God has a plan and a purpose for this. We don't know what it is, but we don't have to. He has it covered."

Unlike Lynn, my biggest fear in those first days wasn't that I would have to turn away from my own son here on earth. I was scared to death that I was about to lose my son for eternity. I had dreamed for almost twenty years that I would get to spend all of eternity with my wife and kids, together in heaven. But if Greg Jr. was gay, was he doomed to hell?

There are lots of pastors and churches out there that would have condemned my son—along with every other person who wasn't straight—for eternity without a backward glance. But Ed—one of the wisest, most Christlike men I knew—gave us hope that all wasn't lost. His advice that day would drive many of our decisions and actions over the next year and beyond, and it guides much of the advice we give to other parents of LGBTQ children even today.

ED'S WORDS PUSHED PAST my tears and into my soul.

"I don't understand how that's possible," I cried, and then all of my thoughts poured out. "I don't understand how any of this is possible. How can God have a purpose for this? How can my son feel like this? Believe this? We raised him right. He's in a Christian school. He's in church. We've taught him about the Bible and what it says about sin. He accepted Christ when he was eight years old. How can Greg Jr. think he's gay?" I was crying again. "I just don't understand," I repeated, miserably.

In times of crisis and dramatic life change, our reactions often reflect the places where God is still working in our lives. Greg's first impulse, as he's shared, was anger. Mine was guilt. If my son was gay, I thought it must be my fault. For other parents the first response might be denial (*"We're not going to talk about that"*) or depression (*"I've lost my child forever"*).

Ed leaned forward, his voice gentle. "Well, of course you don't understand, Lynn. This isn't a sin that you wrestle with, so of course it doesn't make sense to you. It doesn't have to."

Looking back, that was a double-edged response. On the surface, Ed's words filled me with relief. *Of course* I didn't understand. God didn't expect me to understand. I was free to leave it with him.

It would be months before I stopped to consider another implication of Ed's choice of words. *This isn't a sin that you wrestle with,* he said, insinuating I had my own set of sins to deal with.

And it would be years before I realized that even in his comfort, Ed's words reinforced another idea I'd never questioned: *being gay was a sin.*

I hesitate to bring up that word so early in our story. In our experience, as soon as someone says *sin* in a conversation about LGBTQ issues, battle lines are drawn. Families and churches fracture over those three little letters.

However, I also want to be honest about our story, and this was where we were, spiritually and emotionally, on the day we found out our son was gay. We believed that homosexuality was a sin, and so did our pastor.

Ed Dobson was one of the most loving, generous, and spiritually mature people we've ever been blessed to know. He was also a man whose faith was growing and changing, just like all of ours. Ed's first job in ministry was at the conservative Liberty University, and in the early 1980s he helped to draft the platform of the Moral Majority, the right-wing political arm of the evangelical church that once issued a "Declaration of War" on homosexuality. By the time of our meeting, he had developed mixed feelings, at best, about how the church had politicized certain issues. At the height of the AIDS epidemic Ed was volunteering his church and his service to help the gay community, despite the vocal disapproval of some conservative Christians, even people in his own congregation.

Ed was a dear friend and confidant both for us and for Greg Jr. right up until his tragic and untimely death in 2015. He loved our son, and nothing ever changed that.

That morning, as we were leaving, he hugged us. "God has a purpose for this, but sometimes it will be a hard thing to see. I think it's easier for me to come to terms with my ALS than it will be for you to go through what you're going through."

Ed had only recently shared his diagnosis of ALS (amyotrophic lateral sclerosis, or Lou Gehrig's disease) with the congregation. For him to say this—that God was trusting me with a challenge bigger than the one he had put in his faithful pastor's path—was terrifying. I didn't want a challenge bigger than a terminal diagnosis! I wanted our son to be straight.

Greg

NEEDING TIME TO PROCESS everything Lynn and I had heard, we put off the conversation with our son for one more day. That night we told Greg Jr. that he needed to be home the next night for dinner, because we had some important things to discuss. Though he didn't question what the subject would be, I could see he was curious. And to be honest, I kind of liked making him wait.

Even though it was the only thing Lynn and I had thought about for days, when we went to bed that night we still hadn't developed a specific strategy for how we would confront our son. Our conversations together swung wildly around all the things we wanted to get across. We wanted to discipline him for deceiving us and making us believe he was straight. We wanted to show him how much we loved him. And most of all, we wanted to get our son straightened out (pun intended).

We couldn't sleep. The initial shock of what I saw on my son's computer had worn off, and my anger had faded. In its place, I felt fear. I worried about what people would think of me. I played all kinds of different scenarios out in my head, and ways that my friends and colleagues would question *my* parenting, *my* masculinity, *my* absence in Greg Jr.'s life if they found out about all of this.

The next day went on forever. Each minute felt like hours. The afternoon was unseasonably warm, and when I got home from work Greg Jr. was out on our boat with some friends from school. Lynn and I could hear their laughter drift up from the water until finally, they all filed up the long staircase from the dock. Normally, Lynn would greet Greg Jr.'s friends and offer them snacks or cold drinks, and often invite them to dinner. It was important to both of us to create a place where our kids' friends always knew they were welcome. But tonight we just wanted them to be gone. We weren't going to create a scene, but every minute that passed was killing me. I wanted this conversation to be over.

When the last friend disappeared down the driveway, I turned to my son, who clearly knew something was up. "Mom and I need to talk to you," I said, hearing the stiffness in my own voice. My chest seemed full, and it was hard to breathe. "Let's go outside."

What happened next became a pivotal moment for each of us. We gathered on the deck, high above the river. I didn't bother with small talk when I started the conversation.

"Mom and I found pornography on your computer."

The look on Greg Jr.'s face told me everything I needed to know, but I pressed on.

"Are you—"

"Gay? Yes." Greg interrupted before I could get the word out. His chin was up, and he met our eyes without blinking. There was no apology in his voice. "Any other questions?"

My son was just as brash and defensive as I would have been at his age if I was called on the carpet for something. In that moment, my love for the strong, smart, and quick-witted man he was becoming washed up against my rising sense of panic.

Now what?

Lynn

"GAY? YES." MY HEART broke as those two words destroyed every image I had of what I wanted our family to look like.

He sounded so sure of himself, so confident with his answer. If he was embarrassed he didn't show it, but as his mother, I could look at his face and see the uncertainty behind his stoic eyes. His life, too, had just changed in an instant.

If a child's coming out seems like an earthquake to parents like us, imagine what it's like for our kids, who are acknowledging this big, controversial, polarizing thing about themselves for the first time. According to the Pew Research Center, most gay, lesbian, and bisexual people know by the time they're twelve that they are something other than straight.* For Christian kids, they often struggle with the realization that they aren't going to fit the family's or society's ex-

---

*http://www.pewsocialtrends.org/2013/06/13/a-survey-of-lgbt-americans/.

pectations. They carry the burden alone, working through their own questions.

Now imagine what it's like to find the courage to talk about it.

Years later, we stumbled across a blog series called *Blue Babies Pink* by a gay Christian man named B. T. Harman, who shares his own coming-out experience.* His description of what it's like to be the gay person coming out to their parents was eye-opening:

> Kids have a sense of what their parents dream for them. We hear their conversations growing up. We see how they talk about our older siblings and their spouses and their kids. And kids also have an innate sense of wanting to please their parents, of wanting to make them happy. We start doing it from a young age, and I bet even when we are old and gray, we'll still want to please them.
>
> This is the dilemma for the gay child.
>
> We know there is a dark moment sometime in the future where we will utterly crush our parents, where we will walk in the room and force-feed them the biggest serving of disappointment they could ever imagine. And it will be our doing, not because we want to, but because we have to. We have to reveal that we aren't like them. We have to reveal that there has been an invisible minority in their midst.

---

*You can read Brett's whole story at www.bluebabiespink.com.

Greg

THAT AFTERNOON ON THE deck, I wasn't thinking about what an important moment this was for my son. I wasn't thinking about what he needed. I was still thinking about myself.

How had Greg Jr. hidden something so important from me? How had he chosen to do something that was so clearly against everything I'd taught him?

When a child comes out (or, as Greg Jr. likes to put it, is pulled out) of the closet, they are in one of the most vulnerable moments of their lives. Telling the truth, especially if they expect a negative response, takes an enormous amount of courage.

And all they want from us in return is our love.

I've heard a lot of coming-out stories in the last twenty years, and in every one of them—no matter how brash or confident the person was about their sexuality—the thing they all longed most for was their parents' support. But all too often that's not what parents offer.

Lynn

I WAS HEARTBROKEN. BUT more than that, to be honest, I was embarrassed. I always thought Greg and I had strong, positive, open relationships with our kids—the kind of relationship I never had with my own family. This changed everything.

"How do you know?" I pleaded with him, jumping straight from the "denial" to the "bargaining" part of grief. "Maybe you're not gay. Maybe you're . . . bisexual!" In the moment, somehow, I thought that would make it better.

Today, Greg Jr. says that he agreed with me. Sure, maybe he was bisexual, he said, trying to pacify me. But all I remember is him shaking his head, cutting off the last bit of hope I had for that perfect, normal life.

"Well, how do you know?" I pressed.

"How do you know you're straight?" he shot back. That's a question that he and many of his gay friends whom we've met over the years are forced to ask often, and I've learned to appreciate their point. How do we *know* we're straight? And why do we expect someone who's gay to have a different way of *knowing*?

But that afternoon by the river, I wasn't ready to think about it. "Maybe you're just confused." I searched my memory for an argument to make. "You had a crush on Brooke at school, and we know that you kissed Connie's friend Kristin." Our older daughter, now away at college, could never keep a secret, especially if it was about her brother. "You wouldn't kiss a girl if you were gay."

Greg Jr. just shook his head.

"I always knew this day would come. I'm just sorry you had to find out now," Greg Jr. said, and for the first time I thought he did look a little bit sorry.

"What's special about now?" I asked him. I couldn't imagine that there would be a "right" time to find out my only son was gay.

He shook his head again. "I didn't want to tell you until after I was done with college."

"What does college have to do with any of this?" I asked, truly baffled.

"My gay friends told me that when their parents found out about them they were totally cut off. Their parents wouldn't pay for college. Some of them got kicked out of the house. And I really wanted to go to college."

My heart, already breaking, tore a little bit more. Our son thought we would abandon him, that we would cast him away. And his belief wasn't completely unfounded. The LGBTQ community is full of stories of kids who have been pushed away from their families. Forty percent of all homeless youth are LGBTQ, and family conflict is the most common cause. More than a quarter of the teens who come out to their parents are thrown out of their homes, at least temporarily.*

Driven by anger or shame, the knee-jerk reaction of too many parents is to punish. "You're off the family payroll," one angry father told his son. Others take away cars, phones, and education. They push their child away, saying "you're no longer welcome in this house." The result is almost always a fractured relationship that separates a child from their parents' influence, as well as their love, for years.

How did my child not understand that I could no sooner turn him away than I could cut out my own heart and say I didn't need it?

---

*True Colors Fund, https://truecolorsfund.org/our-issue/.

Greg

I DON'T REMEMBER WHO answered, whether it was me or Lynn, or maybe we both spoke at once. "This has nothing to do with college," we assured him. "Of course, we'll still pay for your education." I leaned forward and met his eyes. "Your mom and I love you, and we always will. Nothing you do could ever change that. You could even murder someone and we would always love you."

I meant well when I said it, but yes, I implied that being gay was equivalent to murdering someone.

And anyway, even as I said the words, something else struck me. *Greg Jr. had already talked to his friends about this. Someone else knew about our son's sexuality before we did.*

My gay friends . . . That casual reference left me flat-footed. I didn't know that my son had gay friends. Lynn told me later that she suspected that a couple of the guys who came over sometimes might be gay, but she never dared to ask. We'd been living in denial for a long time, and that meant our son had been on this path for a long time without us.

This, for me, became the real issue. Or maybe it was just the issue I could face right then. *Why hadn't he told us?* Our son intentionally led us to believe that he was straight. Later, he admitted that he'd asked one of his female friends to act like a girlfriend when we were around, to throw us off. He'd hidden something from us! He'd lied to us by not sharing what he knew about himself.

When we share our story with others, many people are surprised by this point. Did Lynn and I really expect our seventeen-year-old son to tell us everything, even more than he told his friends? The honest answer is yes, we did. Compared to most families, we were unusually close. Lynn and I had dedicated ourselves to our children, and to making a stable, safe home life for them. We felt like we had a great relationship with our kids, and to find out that one of them was hiding something this big was a huge betrayal.

So, in that moment, sitting on that deck, I was full of self-righteousness. I wasn't thinking about all the struggles, or questions, or corners of my own life that I hid from my wife, let alone my children. I never once put myself in Greg Jr.'s shoes to consider how he would have told us what he knew about himself, considering the legalistic environment we'd created.

Lynn and I could barely stand to let our children hear the word *gay*, let alone have a thoughtful conversation about it. Taking a cue from the "family values" teachers we heard on the radio and read in the books popular at the time, we reinforced to Connie and Greg Jr., over and over, how different we were from "the world" and "those people." If the TV show *Will & Grace* was on, we would make some kind of comment about how "disgusting" it was and change the channel. If we saw a story in the newspaper about a gay couple, we felt like we had to stop and explain to our impressionable kids that *those* people were trying to destroy God's plan for *our* lives.

Why would Greg Jr. ever tell us that he was one of "those people"?

But those thoughts came later. In that conversation, all I

could think about was that Greg Jr. told us that he had priori-
tized going to college over being honest with us.

And so instead of reaching out to my son, I told him in no
uncertain terms that he was grounded—not for being gay, but
for lying about it. And he was losing computer privileges in-
definitely because of the porn. The chat rooms were going
dark. I used the classic parent lines: "Because you violated our
trust, you're going to have to re-earn our trust," and "Life as
you know it is over."

Then, for good measure, I said the thing I most regret:
"We need to get you fixed."

Key Learnings: Make It Personal

+ If you think your child might be LGBTQ but he or
  she has not come out to you, don't ignore it, but don't
  rush into a reaction, either. If you decide to initiate a
  conversation with your child, wait until you're emotionally and spiritually ready to have it.

+ Find someone to counsel you. For us, it was our pastor, but it could also be a mentor, Bible study leader,
  therapist, close friend, or family member. What's important is that it's someone who will respond with
  grace and love, not judgment, and who will help you
  sort through what you're thinking.

+ If your child initiates a conversation and comes out of
  the closet, choose your words carefully. Consider the
  painful statements throughout this chapter and try to

avoid them. Avoid giving ultimatums or making extreme statements in the heat of a moment. Once the word leaves your lips, it's almost impossible to reel it back in.

+ Your child has probably been thinking about this for a long time. Remind them, though, that their news is very fresh for you. It's better to ask for time to process and come back to the conversation when you're ready than to let it get out of control.

+ Offer your child love, no matter what. Even if your internal reaction is negative or confused, your child needs the love of their parents. Tell them that you are proud of their honesty and that you are here for them. Remind them that you are always on the same team, and you want what's best for them. To get there will require grace, patience, time, and understanding.

+ When your child says that they are gay, lesbian, bisexual, or transgender, believe them. Don't pressure them to recant or "act straight" just to please you (or God, who is never pleased by hypocrisy or lies). Our children naturally want to please us, but pretending to be what they're not causes a great deal of emotional and spiritual damage long term. Far too many Christian gay men and women have entered heterosexual marriages to please their parents, and those marriages almost always end in divorce and pain for everyone involved.

✦ This is not the time to express your own feelings. As shocking or confusing as it might be for you, remember that your child is in an even more complicated spot. They've just acknowledged, perhaps for the first time, something very vulnerable about themselves. Your job in this moment is to hear them and give them a safe place to share. Save the debates and discussions for later, when everyone's had time to adjust.

✦ Seek a Christlike response. Ask yourself: If Jesus were talking with your child, what would he say to them? Push aside quotes from the media, the "experts," and even your pastor. There will be time later to work through their ideas. But while everything is fresh and vulnerable, follow the footsteps of the Son of God, who extends grace and offers love first.

2

"I Don't Want to Grow Up"

Lynn

BEFORE WE GO FORWARD, let's step back. How did we get here?

Greg and I both grew up in Farmington Hills, Michigan, a quickly growing, middle-class suburb of Detroit that's consistently ranked one of the safest cities in the United States. My home life, though, felt anything but safe. I grew up surrounded by conflict, with parents who were too distracted by their own crumbling marriage to pay much attention to me. I knew they loved me the best way they knew how, but I spent a lot of time tiptoeing around on emotional eggshells.

If there were people in Farmington Hills who were gay, certainly no one was "out." I remember the adults in my family whispering about one of our relatives, a gentle, suspiciously single man who would sometimes visit on holidays. At least once per visit, my parents would ask if he was dating anyone special, but his consistent, awkward response was always "No, not really."

And then there was a guy in junior high school, Bobby, who was always getting bullied on the bus. The older boys would pick on him and call him gay, but I never really questioned what that meant. This was the 1970s, long before things like that were openly discussed. "He likes boys," I remember someone saying to me, as if it was obvious, and I didn't pursue it.

Homosexuality seemed like something to be pitied, but it was something that didn't really affect me. I had other things to think about, like catching the attention of a wild boy racing his dirt bike through my neighborhood.

Greg

I WAS ONE OF those kids in school who sometimes picked on Bobby. During the bumpy bus ride to and from school, I remember watching his whole body shake as kids, mostly guys who were my friends, called him gay and even worse.

Like Lynn, I didn't really stop to think about what "being gay" actually meant. It was just a word to throw at an easy target. Later, when it was my son being bullied on the bus, I thought about those days a lot, and wondered what happened to Bobby.

I was a guy's guy, always playing football, baseball, water sports, and hockey. When I was fourteen years old, I discovered motorcycles, fast cars, and girls. I took my pornography habit, now an addiction, into the real world. I used a fake ID to sneak into topless bars while I was still in high school, and I jumped into bed with as many girls as I could. I even slept with one of my high school teachers.

But then there was Lynn. I first laid eyes on her when I was thirteen, and I was immediately and completely infatuated with her. (I still am.) She was younger than me, though, and we didn't run in the same circles. I never thought I had a chance with her. Then one day, when I was about seventeen, we started chatting, and at some point, she said, "We ought to get together sometime."

I jumped at the chance.

"How about tonight?" She was sixteen then. We married three years later, when I was twenty and Lynn was right out of high school.

I clearly married way over my head. Lynn is gorgeous, smart, loyal, fun to be with, and has a really kind spirit. But we were both very young and had a lot of growing up to do. As she's said, Lynn didn't have a good example of a healthy marriage. My parents loved each other and provided a nurturing household for their sons, but they had their own issues. They were both heavily dependent on alcohol, which made things unpredictable. Lynn and I were determined to do things differently, but we had no idea how to love each other in a healthy way.

So instead, we lived like the kids we were. For the first few years, we had a wild life. There was a lot of alcohol, and a lot of partying. We also fought a lot.

But I stuck with it because I was too proud to quit, and failing at my marriage wasn't an option.

Lynn

THREE YEARS INTO OUR marriage we moved across the state for Greg's job. We were away from our family and friends, and our relationship was failing fast. We decided it was time to have a baby, somehow thinking that would fix our marriage. I quickly became pregnant, but then had a miscarriage.

Losing the baby was devastating, and it caused Greg to question the existence of God. Even if he once existed, Greg told me, God's plans had gone astray, or he fell asleep, or he died.

Greg may have given up on God, but God never stopped loving us, and he didn't leave us in our grief for long. Just a year later, in 1982, we welcomed our daughter, Connie, into the world, and Greg Jr. followed in 1984. Greg and I went from being a young, party-loving couple to the perfect all-American family. I stayed home with the kids, and Greg worked for his family-owned business. We bought new cars, new furniture, new clothes, and anything else we thought would make us happy.

It was everything I thought I wanted, but something was missing. All of our spending just caused a lot of extra arguments. We wanted to be good parents, but it was clear that what we were doing wasn't the way to get there.

Greg's brother, Mike, and his wife, Patty, lived about two hours away from us. We admired how they seemed to have their lives together. I knew that they had become Christians at some point but didn't ask them too much about it.

Mike and Greg worked together as business partners, which meant they spent a lot of time together. Mike sensed that Greg was searching for something in his life after my miscarriage, and one day he asked if he and Patty could come and talk with us about God.

A week later Mike and Patty showed up at our home and spent an afternoon explaining the basic Christian message of salvation: that we are all sinners, and that the only way to get past the guilt and consequences of our sins was to believe that Jesus is the Son of God, recognize our need for his forgiveness, and accept him as our Savior. In Jesus, we would have eternal life.

Everyone was very polite, but Greg said he couldn't buy the part about how we are all sinners. "I never raped or killed anyone," he said, and dismissed the whole conversation.

Suddenly, though, it seemed like everywhere we turned, someone else was talking to us about the importance of having a personal relationship with Jesus. This was the early 1980s, and the evangelical church movement was exploding in Michigan. Despite myself, I was intrigued.

Greg and I started watching Dr. Charles Stanley's *In Touch* program, which broadcast the church services of First Baptist Church of Atlanta. Dr. Stanley's sermons were down to earth, full of applications that Greg and I could see in our own lives, and we started to understand what Mike and Patty had been talking about. This idea of a personal connection with Jesus really appealed to me.

We watched so many of the programs that we started to refer to Dr. Stanley as Charlie, because he felt like a dad or an uncle to us. We had no idea at the time that thirty years later we would find ourselves living in Atlanta, joining a congregation led by none other than Dr. Charles Stanley's son, Andy.

Greg

ON A THURSDAY EVENING in September 1985, Mike called and asked Lynn and me to both get on the phone. I remember he said, "You two are acting like you're Christians. I just need to know—have you accepted Jesus as your Savior?" We both said no.

"Well, what's stopping you?" my brother asked.

By this point, I had a better understanding of sin and the Ten Commandments. Still, I told him it all seemed too simple, and I assumed there must be a catch.

"It's not meant to be complicated," my brother responded.

I tried another argument. "You Christians don't look like you have any fun. I like to drink. I like to smoke. I like to tell jokes."

"Don't worry about that," Mike said. "If you have things in your life God doesn't like, he'll let you know. What God wants is your heart."

It's interesting, looking back, to realize how important Mike's words were to me then. Being a Christian wasn't about how I lived on the outside. It was about how I loved Jesus on the inside—and more important, how much he loved me.

Mike offered to pray with us. Lynn and I looked at each other silently on different extensions (phones had cords back then). I said I'd like that, and to my surprise, Lynn said she would, too. We prayed with Mike, and the rest is history.

We joined a church and threw ourselves into the Christian experience. Lynn and I were like sponges, with Christian talk radio on in the car, Christian programs on TV, and Christian parenting books on the shelves. We'd always been insecure about being good parents, and so we gave ourselves over to the advice of Focus on the Family's James Dobson, and Insight for Living's Chuck Swindoll, and old-time radio preacher Vernon McGee. In their absolute, black-and-white certainty of right and wrong, Lynn and I found the stability that we'd been lacking in our own upbringings. They taught us how to pray for our kids, discipline with love, and teach them the truth of the Bible from their earliest years.

In the late 1980s and early 1990s those popular ministers and parenting experts were also deeply engaged in the social battles of the rapidly changing culture. Wrapped up in their advice about being godly parents were the powerful "us versus them" messages that set up the battle lines between "true Christians" and everyone else who was part of "the world." Unlike my brother, those teachers cared a lot about how everyone lived on the outside. And one of the primary symbols of "the world" was "the gay agenda." *They* were trying to destroy *our* family.

Lynn

I NEVER QUESTIONED WHAT I heard from the Christian media figures of the 1980s and '90s. These were pastors and psychologists—educated, smart, godly people. If they said that a person's orientation was a "preference" and equated homosexuality with pedophilia and sexual abuse, I believed them.*

My acceptance was partly due, as Greg said, to my desire to learn how to be a godly parent. But also, it came because my vague ideas of what "being gay" looked like were based on stereotypes, not real people. I didn't personally know anyone who was openly gay, lesbian, bisexual, or transgender.

The one interaction I had happened in the mid-1980s, not long after Greg Jr. was born, and it still haunts me today. It was the time when a devastating new disease, AIDS, was exploding across the country, especially in the gay community. Everyone was in a panic because we didn't know how it spread. There were plenty of rumors that fed the stereotypes, and as a new, nervous mom, I believed all of them.

Greg's job in the food brokerage business meant that he entertained a lot, and he often asked me to join him for dinner with his customers and clients. I readily agreed. Greg worked with terrific people, and I looked forward to their company. Plus, it was a good chance to get dressed up and enjoy adult conversation after spending most of my day with young kids.

---

* In reality, children are not more likely to be molested by LGBT people, according to the American Psychological Association (http://www.apa.org/about/policy/parenting .aspx), and studies that say otherwise have been widely discredited (http://psychology .ucdavis.edu/rainbow/html/facts_molestation.html).

On this particular evening, Greg brought a customer to our home for appetizers and a drink before going to a local restaurant for dinner. When Greg introduced me to Jim, my first impression was that there was something different about him. Something about Jim's voice, the way he held his body, and the way he shook my hand felt different. And then it hit me. *There was a gay man in my house! With my children!*

We ate the appetizers and chatted. The minutes felt like hours to me.

And then things got worse. Jim asked to use our bathroom. Greg showed him to our powder room as my adrenaline spiked. What if the babysitter used that bathroom later? Or, God forbid, one of my children? My heart raced as I imagined baby Greg Jr. crawling into the room and pulling himself up by the edge of the toilet.

The toilet that *the gay man* had used.

Could this man give my baby AIDS?

When Jim emerged, I excused myself as calmly as I could while shooting dagger looks at my husband for allowing this to happen. In the powder room, I dove under the sink and retrieved some cleaning supplies. I scrubbed and disinfected that little bathroom as fast as I could, not bothering to put on rubber gloves or protect my dress. I had to protect my babies!

Writing this now leaves me mortified, but the story just gets worse.

Maybe Jim had seen my discomfort or even suspected what had happened in the bathroom. Or maybe he just had too many Southern Comfort Manhattans with his dinner. Either way, a couple of hours later I found myself sitting at a table in a dimly lit Italian restaurant as this man leaned forward and started to sing along with the song that the pianist in the corner was playing. His expression was unmistakable. He was singing to my husband!

I was flabbergasted. It was definitely a love song, and I knew that expression in Jim's eyes. I'd never seen anyone hit on Greg so aggressively, right in front of me. And it was a man!

I was disgusted, and I could tell that Greg was, too. I immediately excused myself from the table, saying I needed to check with the babysitter to see how the kids were doing.

Greg saw the anger on my face and followed me to the pay phones.

"Why are you mad at me?" he asked me.

"Why am I mad?" How could he not see this? "You brought a gay man into our home!"

And then I did it. I snapped, "I will never have another gay man in my home. Ever."

Greg

_____

I DON'T REMEMBER SEEING Lynn ever get so angry, and I've given her plenty of reasons over the years to get angry. But she's a ferocious protector of her children, and everything we knew said that we needed to protect our family from anything connected to the gay community.

Truth be told, we sheltered and isolated our kids a lot as

they grew up, surrounding them with carefully chosen, evangelical, *appropriate* people who would reinforce only the messages that we wanted them to hear.

Like most parents, our intentions were good. I'd gotten into a lot of trouble as a teenager with too much freedom, and I wanted to protect Connie and Greg Jr. from those kinds of temptations. And most of all, Lynn and I wanted them to live like Christians—which at the time for us meant following certain rules and avoiding "the world."

Looking back, the language in our house created an environment that was a long way from Mike's words that had first drawn us to Christ. "It's not meant to be complicated . . . what God wants is your heart." Instead of showering our kids with reminders of Jesus' unconditional love, we built walls of fear and avoidance of difference. Although we never said it explicitly, our attitude of superiority and pride—because Christians like us who went to church and followed the rules were better than the sinners who didn't obey God—filtered down to our kids every day. Greg Jr.'s entire childhood was full of messages about "immoral" and "unnatural" choices. The radio that played while he was in the car and the magazines that we left out on the coffee table warned him that "homosexuals" were attacking our family values—and therefore attacking our family itself. They were our enemy, and so was anyone sympathetic to them.

Lynn

I DON'T THINK I ever heard about, let alone met, a person who led a healthy, fulfilled, spiritually active gay life. Those weren't stories shared by the media I trusted. Instead, all I saw were the extreme images of bare-chested men (and women) at colorful gay pride parades. Every example I saw of what I was taught to call the "gay lifestyle" was of someone depraved, lost, and deeply unhappy. I assumed that's all there was. And that's what I shared with my children.

Even if we hadn't discovered, years later, that our son was gay, those messages would have been a mistake. When we labeled a group of people, we made them less human, and therefore less worthy of God's love. We taught our kids that it was okay to feel disgust toward people God created in his image. And we taught them that being anything less than the "perfect" Christian could push them outside God's kingdom.

That's a lot of spiritual pressure to put on anyone, especially a child.

Looking back, I wish I'd spent more time helping my children see that God loves everyone, even those who live differently than we do. That even if someone isn't living according to what we believe is God's perfect plan, they are still part of his creation. I wish that instead of jumping in front of the TV when a gay couple walked across a sitcom stage, I'd sat down instead and asked my kids what *they* thought about what they saw.

Basically, I wish I'd spent more time talking about grace and less time focused on "The Law."

Greg

AS MUCH AS WE tried to protect our children, there were some things we couldn't control, like the kids at Greg Jr.'s Christian school who started teasing him in grade school. There was a bully on the bus, and some kids who would harass him on the playground.

When my fifth grader asked me what it meant when kids called him gay, I fumbled around, not sure what to say. "It's when two men think that they love each other," I finally said. "But it's not good."

Looking back, I wish I'd seen his need to understand his bullies more than my own embarrassment. I wish I hadn't tried to make a black-and-white, right-and-wrong teaching moment—or at least if I had, that I'd pointed out that what was "not good" was the behavior of the bullies. I wish I'd explained to my ten-year-old that regardless of whether a man loves a woman or another man, God loves that person just as much as he loves us, and that he even loves the mean boys on the bus.

But I didn't, and Greg Jr. accepted my answer without asking anything else. He stoically went back to school, but the bullies were clearly taking a toll.

Lynn

WHEN HE WAS A little boy, maybe just seven or eight, Greg Jr. would frequently wake up in the middle of the night crying. "I don't want to grow up," he would wail. I thought it had something to do with the popular toy store commercial that was on TV all the time. The jingle went "I don't want to grow up, I'm a Toys 'R' Us kid," and it could get stuck in your head.

Greg and I would reassure him, over and over, that growing up was going to be great, but that it was still a long way away. We'd tell him that he didn't have to grow up yet. And then we'd leave him there, alone in the dark.

What we didn't know until decades later was that those fears went deep, and they weren't tied to a TV commercial at all. Greg Jr. had seen the movie *Hook*, with Dustin Hoffman playing Captain Hook in his fairy-tale fight against Peter Pan. And as he watched, Greg Jr. realized that he identified most with the Lost Boys.

Our son knew, even in elementary school, that something about him was different. The boys on the playground obviously saw it. What if they were right, he thought, and he grew up to be gay? What if he was always different? What if being gay really was as bad as everyone said? He didn't want that.

He didn't want to grow up.

Even today, I tear up when I think of that little boy facing his own fears of the future that were fed, not dispelled, by the messages he heard in our home.

Greg

THE BULLIES ON THE bus were a problem, but they weren't our first clue that our son was different. I'd known when he was a toddler that Greg Jr. wasn't like other boys, or at least he certainly wasn't like I had been when I was growing up, or like my brother Mike's kids were.

Lynn and I were worried enough to seek the advice of our Christian marriage counselor when Greg Jr. was just three years old. I wasn't even sure how to phrase the question. "Could our son be struggling with being gay?"

The counselor scheduled a time to watch our family interact together, and then reassured us that Greg Jr. seemed completely normal, and it was too early to worry. With two loving Christian parents, she said, he would be fine. She even told us that once he began attending school, peer pressure would "straighten him out."

But still I worried. Greg Jr. would rather play with his sister's Barbie dolls than the trucks and cars we bought and put all over the house for him. He didn't want to roughhouse with his cousins; he'd rather stay inside and draw pictures for his grandmother.

On one hand, I was amazed and filled with love to watch his personality develop. He was so talented. He loved stories and art, and he could entertain himself for hours with pencils and paper. When our friends were all taking their kids to soccer games on Saturday afternoons, Lynn and I were driving Greg Jr. to art classes.

On the other hand, though, as a father I was embarrassed. What was I doing wrong that my son didn't want to do "boy" things? Was I not spending enough time at home? Were we not bonding the way men were supposed to do?

I was working a lot of hours, helping keep our family busi-

ness afloat during some turbulent economic times, but I
made it a point to engage with Greg Jr. whenever I was home.
I'd invite him to play catch, soccer, and T-ball in the backyard.
It was obvious he was only tolerating my intrusion, and for
my sake he would genuinely try to engage in the game, or at
least care about what hand his baseball glove went on, but
sports were clearly not his thing. I'd try to get him into building blocks and playing with toy guns, but again, there was just
no interest.

The reactions of other people stung my pride. Mike had
four kids, two boys and two girls, who were all about the
same age as Connie and Greg Jr. We would get together at my
parents' vacation cabin, and I'd watch his athletic kids tumble
off into the woods to play one game or another, Connie tag-
ging gamely after them. And I'd see Greg Jr. sitting inside
alone.

I was desperate to find things to do with my son. I asked
my friends to include us in their plans. "If you're going to be
doing anything with your boys, please invite us along. Let's
shoot hoops. Let's go camping." But the invitations didn't
come.

Instead, I got a call from Mark, one of my very best
friends who was also a part of our couples Bible study. He
suggested we meet for lunch, and I was happy to agree. I
enjoy meeting people for a meal, and I rarely eat alone. But I
could never get Mark to meet me because of his unpredictable schedule. Now he'd made time just for me. I canceled another appointment to spend time with him.

Over lunch we made small talk, but I could tell he had

something on his mind. Finally, Mark dropped the bomb. "I'm really concerned about Greg Jr.," he told me. "There are certain tendencies in his behavior, and I'm worried he's exhibiting signs that he's gay."

I was floored. Greg Jr. was about fourteen or fifteen at the time, and Lynn and I had never talked to any of our friends about what we'd seen or what we feared. But now it was clear that other people saw what we did.

I could sense his pity. At first I didn't take it well, but as I processed our conversation, I realized how difficult this must have been for Mark to share his concern about something so personal. It was obvious that his concern came from a place of love for my family. Still, I had no idea what to do about it.

Key Learnings: Make It Personal

+ Take an honest look at what you learned and observed about sexuality and gender when you were growing up. The things we heard (or didn't hear) in our own formative years will affect what we pass along to our own children, especially if those perspectives are unexplored. If you were told that being gay or transgender was something shameful, or something to be hidden, you may have a harder time talking openly with your child. If your parents or pastor were outspoken about judging people who were gay, some of that might still seep through in your own behavior.

✦ When you do talk to your kids—straight or gay—about what it means to be LGBTQ (and given the openness of today's culture, you're almost sure to have the conversation at some point), be aware of the underlying messages that certain words and phrases carry. After talking to many LGBTQ individuals and family advocates, we learned to avoid these words and phrases:

✦ Calling someone "a homosexual" or a group of people "homosexuals" sends a message that there's something clinically wrong, diseased, or psychologically damaged about a person.

✦ Referring to someone's "sexual preference" implies that a person's sexual identity is a choice that can be changed as easily as their wardrobe, or a behavior that exists on their surface rather than as part of their identity. There's little evidence that supports the idea that a person's sexual identity can ever change, and many of those who were widely touted as success stories for sexual reorientation later ended their heterosexual marriages and now identify as gay again.

✦ Talking about a "gay lifestyle" implies that all people who are attracted to the same sex live with the same (presumably negative) priorities and values. Just as not all Christians live exactly the same way or prioritize the same things, not all LGBTQ people believe or express themselves the same.

✦ The "gay agenda" is a phrase used mostly
by conservative media figures to create fear
that there is an organized conspiracy of some
kind that threatens heterosexual couples and relationships. We've never met an actual LGBTQ
person who has any agenda to hurt others.

✦ And of course, avoid slurs and derogatory slang
that can't even be printed in a family book like
this. Calling someone names isn't appropriate
for kids in the schoolyard, and it's not appropriate for parents at home, either.

✦ Remember that our kids are always watching our actions. One of the most important things that we, as
parents, teach our children is how to treat others with
respect and love. If we express disgust for another
human being—whether it's a celebrity on TV or a
new neighbor on our block—we show our children
that some people are not worthy of our love and respect. When we describe other people as disgusting,
appalling, horrible, strange, perverted, etc., or when
we shun them and don't talk about them at all, we
contradict God's direct command to love our neighbors.

✦ If your child initiates a conversation with you about
what it means to be gay, answer simply and directly,
without criticizing, in a way that is age appropriate.
Many psychologists encourage parents to answer a

child's question with questions of your own, in order to figure out what they're really asking. When a child says, "What does it mean to be a lesbian?" the best first response is "Why do you ask?" They might be trying to sort out name-calling they heard at school, or to understand why a classmate has two moms. As they get older, their questions get more sophisticated, and you may find yourself exploring the moral and spiritual aspects of sexuality and diving together into what the Bible says. Regardless of what you conclude, always emphasize that each person is God's creation, loved by him.

+ If your child is being bullied, remind them over and over how much they are loved. Help them understand that while bullies might use words as insults, people who are gay are not bad people. Find passages in the Bible where Jesus stands up for people who are weaker or different and never sides with groups that pick on others.

3

"We Need to Get You Fixed"

Lynn

"*WE NEED TO GET you fixed.*" Greg's words hung in the air that summer afternoon on the deck. Clearly something was wrong with our child, and it was up to us, his parents, to make it right again. But how could a parent "fix" something like this?

Greg and I had no idea. Though we'd had a few days to process what we'd learned about our son, we hadn't really talked about the future. Without a plan, the conversation fizzled, and we each retreated to our separate corners: Greg Jr. to serve out his grounding in his now-computerless room, and Greg to his study.

As for me, I went back to hiding in my bedroom, curled up in the fetal position. The fear of what we were facing overpowered me, and I felt physically sick, like I would throw up.

What would happen to my family? What would happen to ME?

To be honest, I spent most of my time on that second question. I wasn't thinking about my son and what our discovery meant for him. I wasn't suffering because of his pain, or even thinking about what he must be feeling now that his secret was out. I was thinking about myself: *my* dreams and *my* pride.

Like a lot of stay-at-home parents, I'd tied a lot of my identity to my kids. It's easy, as a mom, to let our kids' successes become our successes. Their futures become our futures. After my own difficult childhood, I was 100 percent committed to giving my children the perfect, all-American family. But clearly, to me, that couldn't happen if I was the mother of a gay son.

I'm not the first mother to let her own desires for the future interfere with how they understand their children. I did not want to give up my dream of someday being a grandmother to his children or a mother-in-law to his wife. But more than that, I didn't want to be embarrassed or hurt. I was afraid of how my friends and my church would react. How could I face them?

I had navigated a lot of pain in my life, but nothing like this. I was totally unprepared. And so when my child needed me most, I was too busy feeling sorry for myself to be there for him.

Instead, I prayed for hours, begging God to make this go away. *God, I don't want this! Give me my old life back!*

WHEN I SAID "WE need to get you fixed," what I meant was "We need to make you heterosexual." I wanted Greg Jr. to be well adjusted and happy, which to me meant that he needed to be straight. I was convinced that all gay men lived miserable, depraved lives, and I didn't want that for my son.

But even as I dictated that my son needed to change, a small voice in the back of my head reminded me that it wasn't up to me.

At the time, Lynn and I had more than twenty years of marriage under our belts. And for more than half those years, we'd been in couples counseling, working on the issues in our relationship. Most of those issues came from us trying to change each other—which really was me trying to change Lynn. It took a long time, but by the time we found Greg Jr. out, even I'd figured out that I can't change another person. It was hard enough to change things I didn't like about myself.

Plenty of counselors, books, and life experience had taught me that only God could change a person. He could convict, he could motivate, and he could redirect. But me? Thinking that I could make Greg Jr. straight was an exercise in futility.

And yet I couldn't give up. The way I saw it, it was my job as a dad to get Greg Jr. to the places where God could change him.

So, I called in the big guns. I needed professionals who could lovingly show Greg Jr. that he was making a bad decision.

I still had so much to learn.

Lynn

THE IDEA OF TURNING to trusted experts wasn't new to us. Just a year or two before we found Greg Jr. out, Connie had developed a full-blown eating disorder. She was in high school at the time and tormented by this false image of herself she saw every time she looked in the mirror.

The best thing that Greg and I could do to help her was to surround her with a team of wise people. She had a psychologist and a nutritionist, and at one point we even brought her to a faith healer. And over time, and under their care, it worked. She was healed.

So, when it seemed to us like our son needed help "working through his issues," Greg was ready to take the same approach.

Because to us, at the time, being gay was Greg Jr.'s struggle just as anorexia was Connie's. It was something Satan put in his path to derail him from the life God wanted him to have. "We need to get you fixed" really meant "You made a bad choice, but we can put you in front of people who understand the errors of your choice, and with them you will have the opportunity to rethink your choice."

Greg

WE SENT OUR SON to talk to some of the smartest, most trustworthy, most biblically grounded men we knew. That summer, Greg Jr. met with Pastor Ed and with a Christian therapist, a friend with doctorates in both theology and psychology who often counseled Lynn and me. We also arranged for him to talk with another outstanding Christian pastor whom we had a personal relationship with and whom we trusted, and so did Greg Jr.

We were fortunate—far more so than many parents who find themselves in our position—to have such a great group of godly, compassionate advisors who already knew us, and who we knew we could trust to respond to our child with compassion.

Lynn

SADLY, MANY PARENTS WHO find themselves in our position, struggling to know how to respond to an LGBTQ child, don't have a safe landing zone within their church. We've heard from many couples who confess that their pastor is the *last* person they'd want to talk to about their child's orientation or gender identity. Perhaps he has been outspoken as a "culture war warrior," or has even condemned the LGBTQ community from the pulpit. It's hard to imagine, then, how that person would be able to show love and compassion to parents working through issues surrounding a gay or transgender child, let alone how the pastor would treat the child themselves.

In more cases, though, the families we work with just don't have a relationship with their church leaders, and don't feel safe launching a first conversation in such a vulnerable moment. They may have been part of a large church for years but have never seen the pastors except when they're onstage.

In today's modern era of cell phone screens and personal apps, it's easy to slide through life without really interacting on a personal level—even at church. We put on our good clothes, tell the kids to be on their best behavior, and for an hour or two a week we try to look like the perfect Christians.

And with all the distractions that works fine . . . until you find yourself in a crisis and need some one-on-one, personal, God-centered support.

Greg

WE WERE DEFINITELY IN a crisis. I called and scheduled the meetings, reminded Greg Jr. to be on time, and then confirmed with him that he'd gone. To his credit, Greg Jr. talked to every person we wanted him to. We never pushed him to reveal how the meetings went, although of course we were curious. At the same time, I think we were scared to know. *What if Greg Jr. didn't decide to change?*

I could believe that I was doing something to fix the situation as long as Greg Jr. was talking to people we had such high regard for, even if those conversations didn't seem to be leading to any visible change in his beliefs or behaviors.

It was only years later, in the process of writing this book, that we asked Greg Jr. what he remembers about those meetings. He told us that each man emphasized that God loved him just the way he was. None of them did anything to "fix" him in the way we thought he needed to be fixed. Instead, they did what I wish I'd done: they pointed our son to Jesus and assured him that he, and they, would be there to listen as he thought through what was next for him.

Lynn

IT'S IRONIC THAT AFTER being given permission to love my son no matter what, I didn't do much with it.

Pastor Ed had assured me I wouldn't have to give up Greg Jr. just because he was gay, but I still struggled with whether that was true. Didn't the Bible say not to associate with men who practice homosexuality? I was sure I'd heard a verse like that. Ed said that it wasn't talking about parents and children, and I trusted his knowledge and ability to interpret the scriptures. But I also knew I was supposed to love and obey God before everything, even my family. In those early, dark days, I was secretly convinced that God would call me the way he called Abraham to put Isaac on an altar. Not that I would literally have to kill my son, of course, but for a long time I believed God would want me to sacrifice our relationship.

In reaction, I withdrew. I was so afraid of what would happen next that I couldn't engage with the present. In our child's moment of deepest need, we weren't there for him. It breaks my heart to say that today, but it's true.

Greg Jr. describes that time as us "living like polite, curt roommates who tried to stay out of one another's way."

Greg consumed himself with a new role at work, traveling three or four days a week and not coming home until late. Work became a refuge for him; he later said that being responsible for thousands of employees was easier than figuring out how to parent one gay son.

Greg Jr. worked at the restaurant as much as possible, and once his grounding was over, he spent time with his friends (although sleepovers with other guys were now out of the question). Meanwhile, I continued to hide in my room. I would come out to make dinner every night, because that's what a "good mom" does, but we ate in silence, or we talked about Greg Jr.'s college plans. For a long time it seemed like that was our only safe subject.

Mostly, though, Greg Jr. was left to process this scary time in his life on his own or with his friends. Looking back, that's the thing that I *should* have been afraid of.

In the years since our son came out, Greg and I have talked to a lot of LGBTQ kids and adults, and we've done a lot of research on what the coming-out experience is like. Most tell us that they were teenagers when they started to share their identity with others. Almost all of them, like Greg Jr., turned first to their friends, other kids without much life experience and whose brains haven't fully developed their decision-making abilities. No wonder the rates of depression, substance abuse, and risky sexual behavior for lesbian, gay, bisexual, and transgender teens are so high. And the suicide rate is heartbreaking. Not only are LGBTQ youth almost 5 times more likely to attempt suicide as heterosexual teens are, but teens who are rejected by their families for their sexual orientation or gender identity are *more than 8 times* more likely to try to take their lives than those kids who have their family's support.* Yet many kids, like our son, don't feel safe sharing their experiences with their parents, or in their churches.

As our friend Dr. David P. Gushee says in his powerful book *Changing Our Mind,* "It says something really terrible when the least safe place to deal with sexual orientation and identity issues is the Christian family and church."

Greg

WHEN WE DID TRY to talk to Greg Jr., we ended up lecturing instead. I told him over and over that he needed to *seek the truth.* What I meant, of course, was that Greg Jr. should read the Bible and see in it what we saw: that homosexuality was not God's plan for him.

Meanwhile, Lynn would slip into what she calls "Bible-preaching mama" mode and read Greg Jr. the scriptures that she thought would show him his sins.

Like most evangelicals, we turned to the seven verses that, in modern English translations, appear to directly address homosexuality. They seemed pretty straightforward to us: "Don't lie with a man as with a woman," we told our

---

*The Trevor Project, "Facts About Suicide," https://www.thetrevorproject.org/resources/preventing-suicide/facts-about-suicide/#sm.0000rn7lfo1zxfiiqqf17qh9221t4.

son, as if he'd never read or thought about the passage himself.

Lynn and I genuinely believed that if Greg Jr. just read the same verses we did and listened to the same "experts" we did, he would see the error of his ways and, well, stop being gay. *Seeking the truth* meant seeing things our way.

Of course, it wasn't that easy. Greg Jr. had been seeking the truth for years. He'd been exploring what it meant to be gay since he was in his early teens. He'd been reading his Bible but also talking to other gay teenagers online, and as soon as he was old enough to drive, he started visiting a gay coffeehouse in a town fifty miles away, where he wouldn't be recognized. He'd even had his first relationship, kissing a guy for the first time when he was sixteen. We had no idea. In fact, we'd innocently taken Greg Jr.'s boyfriend on a family vacation with us not realizing that he was his "boyfriend."

Now, while Lynn and I wallowed and waffled about how to handle this revelation about his sexuality, our son didn't budge. He'd worked through his theology already, and he was ready to dig in and argue. When Lynn pulled out her verses and started preaching, our son shot back, arguing that Old Testament passages referred to idol worship and the specific set of rules that God set for the Israelites—rules that we'd always said were no longer applicable today. After a lifetime of Bible classes in a Christian school, Greg was very well grounded in his theology.

I found one small moment of comfort in this. My greatest fear was for my son's eternal soul, but at no point, even in the darkest days, did Greg Jr. ever deny Christ. He'd prayed with Lynn and asked God for eternal life when he was eight years old. Being gay, he said, didn't change who he was.

Greg Jr. was gay, and he knew that he was going to stay that way. He never signed up to be gay, and he was confident that God made him this way, and we couldn't "fix" him, because he wasn't broken.

Lynn

EVEN AS WE URGED Greg Jr. to seek the truth and punished him for not telling us the truth, as a family we agreed to live a lie of omission.

When I was growing up, my family lived by the mantra "what happens in this house stays in this house." It was important not to expose our dirty laundry even to our church or closest friends.

Now, even as I patted myself on the back for getting Greg Jr. in front of people who could fix him, I fell back into my parents' model of behavior for myself. I feared the judgment and rejection that would surely come if our friends—especially the other people at church—knew how deeply we had failed as a family. And to be honest, I still held out hope that this was something Greg Jr. would grow out of. If this "sexual preference" was just an adolescent phase, it was better if no one but Greg and I knew about it.

This is a common reaction that we consistently hear from

parents. "We'll all go in the closet and hang out until we talk our child out of this, or they realize that this isn't good for them," summarized one dad.

But hiding the truth never makes things better.

I told myself that my secrecy was noble, that I was keeping secrets for my son's sake. Greg Jr. had asked us not to tell our friends because he didn't want people at church judging him or trying to fix him. But really, I held back because I was ashamed. I feared the reactions of people I respected and cared about. I dreaded confessing that I had been a bad parent.

It was a lonely time, different from any loneliness I had felt in the past. On the surface, everything looked normal. I did housework, shopped for groceries, went to Bible studies, and even got together with friends. But being with people was painful.

Greg and I were part of a Bible study with five other couples whom we loved deeply. We'd known and done life together for years. We'd prayed for each other as we went through births, deaths, job losses, illnesses, broken relationships, financial problems, and yes, parenting concerns. Every time we got together that summer, I wanted so badly to tell them that my son was gay, and yet I couldn't bring myself to say the words.

Hiding ourselves was one of the most dangerous, ill-advised things we could have done that summer, and the emotional toll on all of us was huge. God did not create us to do life alone. Satan uses secrecy and fear to break apart the bonds between God's children, and to leave them in places of helplessness and doubt. Sharing our stories with friends and loved ones builds trust, helps us process our experiences, and helps us learn from one another's experiences.

Today, whenever we meet parents who are struggling with their child's identity, the first thing we do is encourage them to tell us their story. Just getting the words out of their heads and into the air makes a huge difference in their perspective.

Greg

IT WAS DURING THAT time, after Greg Jr. was out but before anyone close to Lynn and I knew, that I started to notice how many gay jokes, insults, and slurs people around me used every day.

There was one day, the same week we confronted Greg Jr. about the pornography, when I went to lunch with some of the guys from work. We were at a Chinese restaurant, and one of my colleagues told a joke about gay men. Everyone at the table roared except for me.

I felt like someone had turned a spotlight toward me, and that everyone would notice my changed reaction. Because the embarrassing truth is, if I'd heard that joke a week or a month before, I would have laughed, too. Now it just broke my heart.

When you have a gay child, you suddenly become aware of how often people say things at the expense of others. You start to realize how often you've said similar things, trying to be funny, or how easy it was to overlook people being mistreated when it didn't affect you personally.

Lynn

THINGS AT HOME WERE going from bad to worse. Pastor Ed had warned us not to spend too much time "looking in the mirror" or assigning blame for what was happening, but we did it anyway.

Why was Greg Jr. gay? For years we'd heard pastors and media personalities saying that people become gay as the result of over-nurturing, over-doting moms, and absent, unengaged dads.

In 2001, the same year Greg Jr. came out, Christian psychologist and bestselling author James Dobson published *The New Hide or Seek*, which said this:

> As a generalization, it can be said that homosexuality results from a home life that usually involved confusion in sexual identity . . . the most common home environment of a future male homosexual is a home where the mother is dominating, overprotective, and possessive, while the father rejects and ridicules the child. The opposite situation occurs too, where the mother rejects her son because he is a male. Generally, the same kinds of role confusion in the home contribute to female homosexual tendencies. In some sense, the girl feels rejection because of her gender

and comes to believe only a male identity carries
worth...

The best prevention of gender confusion remains
a strong home life. Homosexuality is much less likely
to occur in the context of a loving home where parents are reasonably well adjusted sexually themselves.
I don't think it is necessary to react with paranoia even
in this aberrant culture. If parents provide a healthy,
stable home life and do not interfere with the child's
appropriate sex role, homosexuality is highly unlikely
to occur.*

Greg and I had been relying on Dobson's parenting advice for years, and we had no reason not to trust him about
this, too. We didn't believe that God created our son gay, and
so clearly it must be something we had done, or some evil influence we'd allowed to slip through.

When we needed each other's support most, Greg and I
focused our energy on fighting, using a battle of words to
cover up the gaping holes in what we thought our lives
should look like. We started pointing fingers at each other.
We often went to bed angry, sometimes in separate bed-
rooms, after sparring back and forth. Our marriage was
crumbling.

I started to blame Greg, sometimes secretly but other
times, when emotions boiled over, to his face. "He wouldn't
be gay if you would have played more sports with him and

---

*James Dobson, "What Is the Cause of Homosexuality?" *The Dobson Digital Library*,
www.dobsonlibrary.com/resource/article/0f184113-ff27-42d0-824c-4792ae56931a.

were home more often!" I accused my hardworking husband of being a workaholic.

Greg fired back, "He wouldn't be gay if you weren't such a possessive and overbearing mom!"

Ouch, that hurt. I knew that I was protective and a perfectionist. I took my job as a mom and household manager seriously, and I would do anything for my kids. But had I done too much? *Was this whole messy situation my fault? Did I encourage him to get dirty often enough? Should I have taken away Connie's dolls when Greg Jr. wanted to play with them?*

Greg and I were both drinking more wine than we should, trying to numb the pain of what felt like a colossal family failure. It never occurred to us, in those early days of silence and tension, that being gay might not be anyone's fault.

Greg

IT GOT SO BAD that one day I considered taking my own life.

It was a clear and sunny afternoon as I drove the 125-mile stretch of interstate from a meeting in Detroit back to my office in Grand Rapids. The weather was perfect, but I was drowning in depression. To Lynn's point, we were both drinking more and fighting daily. Many nights I'd take a glass of wine and a cigar outside to the hot tub. I'd tell myself I was praying, but really I was pouting. I felt like a failure in my marriage, a failure as a dad.

At eighty miles per hour, I approached a bridge overpass. The expansion joints in the concrete highway made a slapping sound against the tires, and I remember thinking it sounded like a rapid heartbeat. As the shadow of the bridge closed in, I was within a millisecond of jerking the wheel and crashing head-on into the bridge support. I wanted to end it all.

Thank God, the millisecond passed, I held the wheel steady, and I avoided a collision. The thought of what I'd nearly done scared the pants off me. I pulled over on the side of the highway. My whole body was shaking as I realized how close I had come to doing the dumbest thing ever. I immediately called my physician, who agreed to see me right away. That day I started a process of self-reflection and medical care.

Lynn

I HAD NO IDEA that my husband had come so close to tragedy.

But then, I didn't know much about what Greg thought or was doing. I was still spending most of my free hours in my room, alone with my grief and with God. Some days I would just cry. Weeks passed, but my heart still felt broken. I just couldn't get past the thought that my son was gay. The truth was there when I first woke up in the morning, and it was the last thought before I went to sleep.

I've never prayed so much in my life. Every day I would beg God to show Greg Jr. his sin and turn his life around. God was so patient with me. He let me pour out my heart over and over again. He let me express my fears for my son, and my embarrassment for myself. He let me stumble through my questions. *Will my son be a victim of a hate crime? Will he contract HIV? Could he die of AIDS? What will my friends think?*

Finally, one day, God decided I'd been in this place long enough. I was lying flat on my face before him, praying the same old prayer. "Please God, show Greg Jr. his sin!" Then something totally unexpected happened.

God spoke to me.

I heard a gentle whisper in my inner conscience that said, "Okay, Lynn, we've been talking a lot about how you want me to show Greg Jr. his sin. Today, let's talk about your sin."

I jumped up, just as surprised as Samuel was in the Old Testament when he heard God's voice speaking to him. *The God of the universe just spoke to me!* It took a few minutes to get over that, and to think about what he'd said.

Let's talk about my sin? What did that mean? I felt like I was a pretty good mom and person. I was doing the right things for my family. I went to Bible study. I took my kids to church. I worked on my marriage.

But in those long, difficult weeks, God had peeled away what I thought was good, and he showed me the truth: I was only looking at my façade, not my core.

On the outside I had all the right things. But what about my heart? Even as I focused on my son's life and begged God to reveal Greg Jr.'s sin to him, I refused to look in the mirror to see some of the messier things God wanted me to see in myself.

My fear of my son coming out as gay uncovered my own sin of pride. I was so focused on the Bible verses that I thought talked about Greg Jr.'s situation that I had forgotten about Matthew 7, where Jesus says, "Why do you look at the speck of sawdust in your brother's eye and pay no attention to the plank in your own eye? . . . You hypocrite, first take the plank out of your own eye."

Well, it was time to get humble. And it was also time to get off the floor and start living again.

Key Learnings: Make It Personal

+ Trying to keep a major life change a secret makes the emotional impact harder to bear. If you have just found out that your child is gay, bisexual, or transgender, find one or two friends or counselors you trust. Saying something—even if you don't know what to say, or the words come out all confused—is better than saying nothing at all.

+ Release yourself and your spouse (or your child's other parent) from guilt. While your world is shifting, you need the support of your family, and casting blame (including on yourself) doesn't help anyone. Nothing that either of you did caused your child to be gay or transgender. Your child is who they are because God chose it, and only he knows why he chose the particular set of physical, spiritual, and personal traits that he did.

+ Acknowledge that you can't "fix" your child. He or she is likely old enough to know their own mind and to have an independent will and self-awareness. Whatever you believe about the cause or morality of your child's sexual orientation or gender identity, who they are is between them and God. Only their Heavenly Father can guide them.

+ If you find yourself sliding into depression, seek medical help. If your child seems to be struggling emotionally or psychologically, seek medical help. This is an incredibly stress-filled time for everyone, as identities and relationships realign, and everyone in the family is at an increased risk for dangerous or self-destructive thoughts and behavior. Seek the support of a counselor or therapist with experience guiding families with LGBTQ members. This is especially important if your child is navigating complicated decisions related to gender dysphoria. The transgender journey is unique in a lot of ways, and there are a lot of new terms and ideas to understand.

+ Don't be surprised if you and your spouse process having an LGBTQ child differently. Each person will work through their thoughts and emotions at different speeds and in different ways. Give each other space, but also focus on the importance of being in this together. The process of adjusting to an LGBTQ child can put a lot of stress on a marriage, and many falter or fail if they're not intentional about working at their relationship.

+ As much as you want to lecture your child and try to create change, remember to also listen. Your child has likely thought about many of the spiritual implications and practical concerns. Take the time to hear them and understand where they are personally.

4
—

Let's Talk About Fear

LIFE OFTEN PRESENTS OBSTACLES and challenges that feel too big to take on. For us, that happened when we found out that our only son was gay. In an instant, it seemed like everything we thought we knew about ourselves, our family, and even our God shifted.

For those difficult weeks, all we could feel was fear.

We're not alone in this. Many of the families we meet, as they process through the discovery that their child is LGBTQ, begin their journey with this same sense of paralysis. Their instincts scream that something terrible or out of their control is happening or is about to happen. Some of them move through those feelings quickly, while others linger in fear for long, heartbreaking years.

This drawn-out fear, as we learned through painful experience, leads to hopelessness, prolongs pain, and ultimately separates us from the God who tells us, over and over, to "fear not."

What Do We Mean When We Talk About Fear?

FEAR, BY MOST PSYCHOLOGISTS' definition, is primarily an emotional reaction to a real or perceived threat, often brought on by a sudden change in situation or perspective.

Fear short-circuits our brains and bypasses our rational thoughts. It goes right for the heart and then shreds our ability to think with a dump-truck load of worst-case scenario images. Physically, fear is the hollow feeling in the pit of our stomach, the heat of shame, or the numbness of hopelessness. When we meet with parents and LGBTQ adults today, we recognize fear in a quivering voice, a tense body, or someone so angry that steam is practically coming out from under their collar.

Fear drives us into the fetal position in dark rooms, where all we can do is pray for the terrible images to go away. It pushes us to numb ourselves with unhealthy substances. We struggle to focus at work or school, and normal routines go unfollowed. When we are consumed with fear, the simplest tasks become overwhelming. Often, that's because our minds are overwhelmed by unanswerable questions about the future.

What will happen when people at church find out? What will people at work say? What will others think about me as a parent?

Then there are the questions about our child. We worry about the potential for hate crimes, AIDS, and loneliness. For many Christians, the fears are spiritual. *Can my child lose her salvation? Will God still love him?*

It's no wonder that fear leaves us feeling as if we're grieving a terrible loss. The future that we once imagined is gone, and things can seem bleak.

Rational and Irrational Fears

IT'S IMPORTANT TO ACKNOWLEDGE that not all fear is bad. God created humans with a fear response so that we could protect ourselves from genuine threats and danger. These are what we call rational fears. We *should* fear things that can physically hurt us.

When we realized that we were the parents of an LGBTQ child, there were rational things we had to learn to consider, especially when it came to our child's safety. We had to come to terms with the truth that a person who is gay, lesbian, bisexual, or transgender is more likely to be a victim of a hate crime than anyone else in America.* From schoolyard bullying to workplace discrimination, our son's path was going to be harder. As his family, we had to learn how to recognize safe people and places and make more thoughtful decisions to protect him.

But irrational fears, as many wise counselors have explained to us, do not create that same sense of heightened awareness; instead, they dig us into despair. Irrational fear is what leaves us frozen, certain that everything will collapse. It pushes us to expect the worst possible outcomes. *My life is ruined. I'll never survive this. When my friends find out, they're*

---

*Haeyoun Park and Iaryna Mykhyalyshyn, "L.G.B.T. People Are More Likely to Be Targets of Hate Crimes Than Any Other Minority Group," *New York Times*, June 16, 2016, https://www.nytimes.com/interactive/2016/06/16/us/hate-crimes-against-lgbt.html.

never going to speak to me again or they will talk about me be-hind my back. Everyone at church will judge me. My child will go to hell.

We can consider our rational fears and make decisions about how to act on them, but when we let a situation consume us, Satan will almost always drag us to a dark, lonely place of irrational fear.

The Urge to Hide

BECAUSE FEAR WAS ORIGINALLY created to be a biological response to physical danger, the human mind often instinctively reacts to fear with a desire to retreat, run away, or hide. This has been true since the first humans, Adam and Eve, felt fear in the Garden of Eden.

After they ate from the tree of knowledge, which God had forbidden them to do, the Bible says their eyes were opened. "Then the man and his wife heard the sound of the Lord God as he was walking in the garden in the cool of the day, and *they hid from the Lord God* among the trees of the garden" (Genesis 3:8, emphasis added).

That desire to hide is still strong in the human DNA, and Satan has corrupted it to isolate us from one another and from our Creator.

Of the many hundreds of parents we know who were faced with the surprise of an LGBTQ child, most reacted at first the way we did, with some form of "let's keep this a secret." Our instincts shouted that we needed to "assess the situation," or get through this latest "phase," or protect something (a sibling or grandparent, a reputation, a job, a future). We told ourselves we were protecting our child, yet the truth is that we were more concerned with trying to protect ourselves.

As our child developed enough courage to come out of the closet, we went into closets of our own. Only later did we understand that the secrecy we insisted on during those early weeks of our journey with Greg Jr. was the worst possible thing we could have done for ourselves, our marriage, our son, and our community.

Satan must rub his hands together with excitement when he fills us with the doubts that keep us in the darkness. Maybe this is a result of the wrong kids influencing him right now. Maybe she's confused and just hasn't met the right boy. We'll just keep this secret and wait it out.

Instead of reaching out to the community that God created to sustain and support us in difficult times, when faced with fear we pulled back and hid our hearts. We shielded ourselves from the very people God put in our lives to help us.

One of the beautiful things about the Christian church is its commitment, generation after generation, to fulfilling the biblical instruction to "bear one another's burdens." When tragedy strikes—whether it's a death, illness, or serious setback—Christians circle the wagons. They visit and provide meals to make sure the affected family knows they are loved.

But when people hide their situation from those who could love and support them, they lock themselves in their closets and grieve the death of their dreams and aspirations for the future alone. On some deep level they may believe Satan's lies that this new development will make them and their children unlovable or unacceptable.*

When we're faced with a major life upheaval, especially if it's something that rocks the foundations of what we believe, the closet (or the dark bedroom, or the over-scheduled work-day, or the unanswered phone) is the worst place to be. As many wise speakers and writers before us have said, nothing good grows in the dark.

In isolation, fear grows. Those worst-case scenarios get even worse, and we react in ways that can leave permanent scars. We've heard fear push parents to lash out in anger to-ward their LGBTQ children and say hurtful, impulsive, cut-ting things. *I can't be near you. I can't support you. I can't love you. God can't love you. It would be easier if you were dead.*

If we linger in the dark too long, we can find ourselves in terrible places. Life begins to feel like a sham. That feeling of hopelessness, like there's no way out, is where lives are lost to suicide and self-destruction.

When we live under the weight of fear, we damage not only our relationships with other people in our community, but also our relationship with God himself, who desires to bring the light of truth into the darkest places of our lives. It's hard to live filled with dread about what might come next and still maintain faith in the God who controls everything.

---

*In too many heartbreaking cases this fear of being rejected by a local church turns out to be rational. Christians aren't perfect, and some congregations don't offer love, grace, or compassion in trying times. If this is the case, a family will need to decide whether this is the best congregation for them overall, but the answer still isn't to hide from the broader church—the body of believers that is bigger than any single church.

What Does God Say About Fear?

GOD TALKS ABOUT FEAR a lot in the Bible. In fact, many pastors and writers say that "do not be afraid" or some variation is the most frequent command in Scripture. Pastor Rick Warren of Saddleback Church says that there are 365 verses in the Bible, one for each day of the year, that teach us to "fear not."*

Clearly, this is something our Father wants us to pay attention to.

But even his repeated assurances that we can "leave all your worries with him, because he cares for you" (1 Peter 5:7) can be difficult, especially for those who were exposed to the idea that God himself is someone to fear. God's perfect plan for us, laid out in Scripture, can come across as nothing more than an impossible-to-keep set of rules, and God's power can make him seem like a guy set on punishing people.

Warren reminds us that ". . . Our hurts and hang-ups can often cause us to think that God is out to get us, that all he wants to do is condemn us and punish us. But that simply isn't true. Jesus is the proof of that."

John 3:17 reminds us that "God did not send his Son into the world to condemn the world, but to save the world through him."

On the last night of his human life, knowing what kind of violence, loss, and radical changes would come in the next twenty-four hours, Jesus paused to reassure his disciples in

---

*Rick Warren, "Don't Be Afraid!" Pastor Rick's Daily Hope, April 28, 2016, https://pastorrick.com/devotional/english/full-post/don-t-be-afraid.

John 14:27: "Peace is what I leave with you; it is my own peace that I give you. I do not give it as the world does. Do not be worried and upset; do not be afraid."

And 1 John 4:18 reminds us that "There is no fear in love. But perfect love casts out fear."

Jesus' desire is to take our fear from us, and to fill us instead with a hope for his perfect future. He did not come to bring wrath and judgment, after all, but to offer himself as an example of perfect love.

What Does It Take to Get Past Fear?

"LET'S TALK ABOUT YOUR sin," God said, and it was a turning point in our family's journey of fear. Why? Because the Lord was showing us that the root of our fear was not only Greg Jr.'s sexual identity, but our own pride.

Irrational fear often comes from the temptation to imagine ourselves at the center of the universe and to consider only our own desires. It separates us from God's purpose and his greater, often invisible plan. It exposes our lack of trust that God has our best interests at heart.

How could God allow this to happen to me? we ask. How could he make such a terrible mistake?

Satan is the father of lies, and his stories can sound convincing. That's why 1 Peter 5:8 reminds us to "Be sober, be vigilant; because your adversary the devil walks about like a roaring lion, seeking whom he may devour."

Getting past our fear begins with getting out of the dark

closet and getting honest with God and ourselves. We may be shocked by the direction our lives and families are going, but he's not. He already knows our fears, and he understands our anger. The book of Psalms reminds us that our God knows the number of hairs on our heads, and that all the days ordained for us were written in his book before one of them came to be. He has a plan, and he knew how your child would fit into this larger plan. He truly is in control, and he's waiting for you to believe that, too.

If you are in a place where your life has been disrupted, and you're currently living in fear, know that whenever you're ready to bring fear to God, he will take it. He will help you sort Satan's lies from the truth, and he will be there to help you lean into your grief.

Because let's be clear: Letting go of fear doesn't mean you won't still grieve what you lost. You had a certain vision and plan for your future, and that has changed. You imagined smooth sailing along well-charted, popular waterways, and now you're in a new place. Moving past fear and trusting God with your future doesn't mean you haven't lost something. But grief is an active journey toward embracing your new normal, and paralyzing fear only delays it. Entering your pain is the first step to healing and hope.

Psalm 34 reminds us that "The Lord is close to the brokenhearted and saves those who are crushed in spirit."

Allow yourself to be devastated. Sit in the feelings for a little while. But when the feelings turn to fear, or the "what if?" questions leave you feeling hopeless about the future, remember that God is a God of hope, and he has a reason for what's happening.

The Enemy wants us to worry about the future and dwell on the past. That's because when we live in the present God is right there with us.

Part 2

SURVIVING

5

—

"What Must It Have Been Like for Him to Grow Up in Your Home?"

Greg

AS IT TURNED OUT, we didn't keep our "family secret" for long. As Greg Jr. started his senior year of high school, only a few of his closest friends knew his orientation. But the bullies had never gone away, and now that he didn't have to worry about us finding out and cutting him off, Greg Jr. quickly got sick of staying ahead of the gossip and abuse. As he puts it, he "outed" himself at school the first week of his senior year by basically saying "This is me. I'm gay. Deal with it."

He didn't tell us that he'd done it, though, and for a long time no one else told us, either. Looking back, what I realize is that Greg Jr.'s big announcement didn't cause much of a stir among his peers, even in a Christian school in a conservative corner of our country. For millennials like them, knowing someone was gay just wasn't as shocking, or life-upending, as it was for Lynn and me. The bullies still picked on Greg Jr.

His friends still supported him and stood up to the bullies, and teenage life went on.

The school administration, on the other hand, was not so accepting. When the vice principal heard what Greg Jr. was saying, she called him into her office and confronted him. "You can't tell people you're gay," she said, "or we'll call your parents."

Greg Jr. was defiant. "Go ahead. My parents already know," he told her. She never followed up with us, and he didn't tell us about the conversation until long after he'd graduated.

Eventually, Connie heard rumors from a few of her friends who were still in school, and she told us that our "family secret" wasn't so secret anymore.

I don't remember being angry at Greg Jr. for telling people, but it definitely got my attention. His choice to go public changed everything, not just for him, but for Lynn and me. "If you're telling your friends," I told him, "we need to be telling our friends."

Lynn

AS HARD AS IT had been to keep our secret, I was sure that telling people the truth about our family was going to be even harder. While we held Greg Jr.'s secret, I could pretend that we were still in control of how people saw our family. Opening up and sharing our truth with others meant giving up that control, and I wasn't ready for that. I wasn't ready to trust that God knew what he was doing.

Not only did God know what he was doing, he also knew that we needed a little shove in the right direction.

While in our self-imposed closet, Greg and I had tried to get ahead of our "problem" by thinking through countless variations of how others would respond if they learned the truth about our son. Ultimately, this produced nothing for me but more fear and anxiety. My mind fixated on the harshest examples I knew of churches and families that shunned their prodigal children and cut off all communication with those who lived outside what they saw as God's rules for right living. In my fear, I was sure that we would all be condemned.

Who could we trust? How much fallout would there be with our family and friends? Would there be consequences in Greg's professional life? How would people treat Greg Jr.? Would we still be welcome in our church?

I expected the worst. I thought everyone we loved would say out loud the things we secretly thought: That we had failed as parents. That none of us could be Christians.

Greg

LYNN AND I DECIDED to go first to two of our closest friends, Jan and Jerry, a couple who had mentored us for many years. They'd raised six kids of their own, and we knew they loved us and loved our children.

We met them at a local restaurant where we ate often. I'm sure they felt the tension in the air as soon as we sat down, but they waited patiently while we made small talk. Finally, I told them we had some devastating news to share. Lynn started to tell them the story of our past few months. The lump in my throat grew, and the tears started to fall down her face. She almost couldn't get the words out.

"Greg Jr. is gay."

In the years since, we've sat with countless couples who have told us these same words about their child. Some of them haven't told anyone else before. And every time, I see the expression that I must have had that night.

Will this person think I'm a bad parent?

Will they think that I have somehow ruined my child?

Will they think less of my child, whom I love even more than myself?

This is what true vulnerability is. It's putting yourself and your story out on the table, not knowing what the response will be.

We knew Jerry and Jan would be two of the safest people to talk to, but still, my stomach was in knots. I was scared they would judge us as bad parents. I was even more worried that they would think less of Greg Jr.

But none of that happened. Jan reached out and hugged Lynn while she cried. Jerry prayed for us, right there at the table. Their eyes showed nothing but compassion. They affirmed many of the things that Pastor Ed had told us about how to pursue a Christlike response.

"God loves you," Jerry said that night, "and he loves Greg Jr."

Sharing our story, we learned, was one of the most healing things we could do. *Why had we waited so long?*

Lynn

NOT LONG AFTER THAT, I sat down with my friend Becky. It was the first time I'd talked about Greg Jr. without Greg with me for support, and I was terrified. Despite the love that Jan and Jerry showed us, I still expected everyone to call me out as a failure as a Christian mother.

But Becky's response was beautiful, a real gift of compassion. Her eyes filled with tears as soon as mine did. She listened intently as I talked, and she asked questions to probe deeper. *How do you feel about this? How does Greg feel?* With each question and each squeeze of my hand, I felt relief. While I knew that Becky had pretty traditional views about sexuality, she didn't judge me or my family. She didn't pretend to have answers. Instead, she shared my pain. She let me process out loud what I was thinking.

After that conversation, I told Greg I was ready to talk to our Bible study. We'd been through a lot with these five fabulous couples over the past decade, and keeping our secret from them, week after week, had been especially hard. And so the next time we met, Greg and I shared what was happening in our lives and in our family. Again, we were met with kindness and love.

The thing that stands out most from that conversation is that what seemed like a shocking revelation to us didn't really surprise the people who were close to us. Our Bible study friends had been part of our family for years, and Greg Jr.'s coming out didn't change that. In fact, it was clear to us now that they'd seen the signs that Greg Jr. was different from other boys. But other than that one awkward conversation Greg had with Mark a few years before, they'd lovingly waited until we were ready to bring them the story.

With every conversation, some of the weight that had been weighing me down lifted, and I started to realize that the shame of the past few weeks had come mostly from inside me. Now that I was building a community of support around me, I was starting to get my feet under me again. As Ecclesiastes says, "a cord of three strands is not easily broken."

Greg

AFTER WE TOLD OUR Bible study, we gradually told others as it seemed appropriate. Not everyone around us offered unconditional love and support. Some people seemed uncomfortable, especially church friends and some family members who had spent the last decade hearing the same Christian media messages we did. We noticed that some friends who used to hug Greg Jr. when they saw him now literally kept him at arm's length, as if he had some kind of contagious disease. Others stopped talking about him altogether, as if he'd died.

It was frustrating, and sometimes infuriating, to watch. Here were people who said they loved us, but they didn't see that the best way to love us was to love our children. I'd have given my eyeteeth (or all my teeth, for that matter) to have just one person from our church family take Greg Jr. by the hand and say, "I just want you to know that I love you, I don't judge you, and I am here for you anytime."

Martin Luther King Jr. once said, "In the end, we will remember not the words of our enemies, but the silence of our friends." That turned out to be painfully true. With just a few exceptions, the silence that surrounded our family during Greg Jr.'s senior year was deafening. Lynn and I probably confided our situation with a dozen people we knew well. Between them and the families at the school, we were sure that our news had spread through our church congregation and local community. Grand Rapids often felt like a small town, where everyone knew everyone's business. But with the exception of a few close friends, almost no one sought us out to ask about what we were going through.

In defense of our friends, I always understood that their silence wasn't the same as condemnation. Most people in our community just had no idea what to say. Homosexuality isn't a topic that people in circles like ours talk about—at least, not in personal, compassionate, vulnerable ways. Our friends, like us, had heard the impassioned rants against the "agenda" of liberal elite homosexuals, but they probably had never loved an openly gay person, either, much less heard their story.

Plus, it's just not easy to enter someone's life when they're in turmoil. Back in the 1980s, Lynn and I had trained to be deacons in our church. One of the things they taught us was how to act when we represented the church at funerals and hospital visitations. "It's your presence that matters, not what you say," the pastor said. In fact, he told us that it was better for us to not say much than to try to offer answers to difficult situations. A hug and an "I'm so sorry you're going through this" would be plenty.

Now it was me facing a crisis, and I felt very much alone. Our church community's silence was devastating to me.

Lynn

IN THE ABSENCE OF understanding, Greg and I continued to notice the other messages in the culture around us. No one in our church or community ever came out and said that our son was going to hell, but the pastors and "family experts" in Christian media didn't give up their messages of condemnation against the "gay agenda" or the "homosexual lifestyle," either.

At one point, Greg and I took a weekend off to go to a popular marriage conference. Our relationship had taken a beating, and we needed a chance to let go of our concerns about Greg Jr. and focus on each other for a couple of days.

That plan was shattered within minutes of the program starting, when the famous Christian couple onstage made a joke that was aimed at the gay community. Most of the audience laughed, and my heart dropped. I looked at Greg, and we just shook our heads.

Did the speakers not realize that in an audience this big that there would be people with LGBTQ family members or friends? Or did they assume that since this was a Christian event, no one in the audience would have, or admit, compassion for the gay community?

Even harder than witnessing the cultural messages was absorbing the thoughtless comments from those who were close to us. I sat in Bible studies while women whom I considered friends complained about the loss of "family values" and the "heresy" of Christian leaders who reached out to marginalized communities. More than once, they lumped "the homosexuals" into their list of things that were threatening their existence.

I'd been saying those same things for years, but now I wasn't so sure. It was a fine line to walk; I still wished with all my heart that my family didn't have personal experience with this, but we did, and it made me understand that not all gay people were depraved individuals trying to destroy the Christian church. At times I felt I had to speak up. "Hey, can we be a little more compassionate here?" Sometimes people apologized. Other times they didn't. And there were times when I didn't speak up but probably should have. I was just starting to understand what a constant battle it would be to live between the church and the gay community.

Greg

AS PASTOR ANDY STANLEY says, "The further away you are from a problem, the simpler it seems. But the closer you get, the more complex it gets." Well, we were right in the middle of a situation, and we didn't have many answers. But others sure did, and some of the sharpest, most painful opinions came from those closest to us.

I'd just come home from another long day at work when the phone rang. It was a family member who sounded furious.

"Do you know what your son is saying about himself?" my relative demanded. Apparently, someone he knew had stumbled across a website where Greg Jr. had publicly stated his orientation as gay.

What made it worse was that Lynn and I hadn't yet told our families what we knew about Greg Jr. To be honest, we'd been procrastinating or outright avoiding a few conversations, including this one, that we anticipated would be difficult.

As it turned out, we'd been right to be concerned. "You'd better get him under control," my relative snapped. That was all it took for my own temper to flare. I slammed down the phone and stormed away.

Never mind that Lynn and I were desperately trying to control this whole situation, or that not so long ago I'd said in no uncertain terms that I would "fix" my son. No one else had the right to judge my family like that.

That conversation shook me out of another layer of my fear and avoidance. In the years since, Lynn and I have met a lot of parents whose initial negative reactions to their LGBTQ child ran up against their parental protectiveness when their children were attacked.

For example, I have a friend who works in a very masculine industry. For years, he listened to his coworkers mock and criticize the gay community, all the time knowing that his teenage son was gay. This dad never acknowledged his LGBTQ son to his coworkers, deciding that it wasn't safe for him (or his son) to be out. The father-son relationship, meanwhile, strained to the breaking point.

But then the dad's mother—his son's grandmother—sent

the boy a scathing letter, tucked inside his birthday card. She basically disowned her own grandchild and talked about what a disappointment he was. It was devastating for the son, but it catapulted the dad into action. Today he's a staunch and vocal supporter of his son, and their relationship has reached new heights.

In another family, it was a nosy aunt who pushed the family to take a stand. After years of family gatherings with this relative asking her nephew, loudly, if he had a girlfriend yet or why he wasn't dating, the father finally pulled his sister aside and told her to stop with her questions, because his son was gay and was going to stay that way. It was the first time he'd acknowledged it out loud to anyone.

Lynn

WITH EACH INTERACTION, POSITIVE and negative, God was shifting us a little. He was bringing us past our fear and into a place where being Christians with a gay son was our new normal. This was our life now, and it was time to figure out how to live it.

That doesn't mean we liked it. To be honest, Greg and I still didn't want any of this. We were going through the motions, but we prayed every day that God would change it. Having a gay son felt like a trial that we were being called to suffer through.

One night, we were standing in the foyer of our house, chatting with our close friends Doreen and Mark before Bible study. Greg said something about Greg Jr., and Doreen shook her head.

"Oh my gosh," she said. "What must it have been like for him to grow up in your home?"

We all froze when she said it, Doreen most of all. It was obvious she hadn't meant to be so blunt. She and Mark really loved us, and Greg Jr., which is what drove her words, not a condemnation of us.

But Doreen's honesty would prove to be one of the very best gifts that anyone has ever given us, because for the first time, I stepped back and saw what she saw.

What had it been like for Greg Jr., knowing what he knew about himself, to sit in our home while we criticized gay couples on TV? What was it like to listen to us unintentionally judge him, and call him names, and act as if he was unforgivable? And how had he felt for the last few months as he carried the weight of being an openly gay person in the church while Greg and I were absent and self-focused?

The conclusion rocked my soul: we hadn't been safe for our son, and we still weren't.

Greg

WHAT CREATES A SAFE family environment? We've done a lot of thinking about this, and it always comes back to those lessons we learned while boating. Lynn and I have always believed that one of our jobs as parents is to create a harbor where our children, even after they're grown, can come to get rest from the storms of life that they encounter. In a safe family, each person can trust that their confidences and truths will be protected and will not later be used against them as emotional weapons. We want our children to trust that we are always looking out for them, even if we don't always agree on everything. They should always know that, no matter what, they are loved.

That was our goal, but Doreen's words set us on our heels and made us realize that somewhere along the way, we'd gotten way off track.

We knew we loved our son. We would do anything for him. But had we shown him that? Or had we been subconsciously communicating a belief that God had somehow made a mistake with Greg Jr.? We'd been focusing so much on what we thought was *wrong* that we'd lost sight of what God had made *right*.

Charles Swindoll famously once said, "You want to mess up the minds of your children? Here's how—guaranteed! Rear them in a legalistic, tight context of external religion, where performance is more important than reality. Fake your faith. Sneak around and pretend your spirituality. Train your children to do the same. Embrace a long list of dos and don'ts publicly but hypocritically practice them privately . . . yet never own up to the fact that its hypocrisy. Act one way but live another. And you can count on it—emotional and spiritual damage will occur."

The Bible is clear about this. Our children—male and female, gay and straight—are God's creations. No matter what we may think of their choices, their very existence is never a mistake, because God doesn't make mistakes. God creates beautiful people who each reflect his image in some unique and special way.

Lynn

GOD WAS LOOSENING SOMETHING in my heart and opening a small window of normalcy between me and my son. Still, as the initial shock of our new life wore off, my "Bible-preaching mama" moments actually increased. I pulled out the Bible verses every chance I got and tried to guide Greg Jr.'s spiritual life in the ways I thought it should go.

I was not going to give up my son's soul—and that's what it felt like was at stake—without a fight. As a Christian, I believe that we will all live for eternity, and I want to be sure my husband, my children, and I spend it together in heaven.

This concern for our children's spiritual lives is something we encounter with most of the Christian parents we meet. Sure, as parents we worry about our children's physical safety. But mostly, we worry about their souls. I prayed regularly that both Connie and Greg Jr. would desire their own relationships with the Lord as they transitioned to adulthood. I probably mentioned those prayers too often to Greg Jr.

It worried me that he'd stopped going to church after people there found out about his sexual orientation. (He later explained that he was working so that he could save as much money as possible, in case Greg and I backed out of our agreement to send him to college. This was his Plan B if we cut him off.)

Finally, about a year after we first found out he was gay, Greg Jr. and I were walking on Oak Street in downtown Chicago, and I was telling him again about how I was scared he would turn away from God. He'd been hurt by so many Christians at that point that I couldn't see how his faith would hold up under the pressure.

Greg Jr. stopped in the middle of the sidewalk. He took my shoulders and turned me to face him. "Mom, I am totally offended by that comment."

I was flabbergasted. "Why?"

"Because I would never do that. I *would never turn* away from God."

He stared hard at me, and I backed down. "That's good to know," I said. "I'm sorry for offending you." We kept walking, and neither of us said anything else about it.

In my heart, I was singing, dancing, and celebrating. God wouldn't give up on his creation, and my son wouldn't give up on God. For the first time in a long time, I thought that this would all be okay in the end.

Greg

BY THE TIME GREG Jr. and Lynn had that conversation, he'd finished high school and had gone off to college. After some deliberation, he'd chosen DePaul University in the heart of Chicago, about a three-hour drive from home.

Greg Jr. was excited to start over in a big city, and to be honest, Lynn and I were relieved when he left. There had been a time when we worried about having an empty nest. We'd talked about how hard it would be to not see our children every day. But God designed families so that sons and daughters would eventually leave their fathers and mothers, and by the time it happened, we were ready. Things had been tense in our home for far too long.

Greg Jr. was eager to test his independence. My relationship with Lynn was stressed, and our son's presence was a constant reminder of how we thought we'd failed as parents.

When we dropped him off at his new college apartment and drove away, I think we all breathed a sigh of relief.

Key Learnings: Make It Personal

✦ Tell your story. This doesn't mean you should start broadcasting every detail of your family's journey on social media or sharing personal details with everyone you talk to. It's also important to provide a safe, confidential space for your child to process their journey. But as soon as possible, start to include people who are safe for you: friends, family, and mentors.

✦ Pray about how and when to open your experiences up to others, including your child's younger siblings or other family members. Each situation is different, so don't feel pressured by anyone else's timeline.

+ Think about the things you most want to hear in these moments of vulnerability. Tuck them away and use them when someone in your circle faces a challenging season of their own. For us, we weren't looking for deep theological insight or perfect answers. We just wanted to know that we'd been heard. We longed for words like:

> + I love you, and I love your family.

> + I am not an expert on the questions you're asking, but I'm here to work through them with you.

> + How are YOU doing today?

> + How can I pray for you today?

> + Is there anything I can do to help your child process what they're feeling?

+ Offer grace to the people who respond awkwardly to your significant life change. They may be worried about saying the wrong thing, which leaves them saying little or nothing. Or at some point they may make a thoughtless joke or comment. Remember that this situation is new for them, too. Just as your child had been processing their truth for a while before you found out, now you're the one who has had time to reflect, and the person who's listening is trying to catch up.

+ Some friends, family, or church members may react not just awkwardly, but with outright anger or condemnation. They may confront you or your child with Scripture or cut your LGBTQ child out of events. Approach these situations prayerfully. You may need to agree to disagree or to establish boundaries to protect you and/or your child from an unsupportive person. In extreme cases, you may need to distance yourself and your family entirely from people or places that are toxic mentally, spiritually, and potentially even physically. Ask:

    + Is our church a safe and healthy environment where our LGBTQ child can grow in their relationship with Jesus? If not, find one that is.

    + If we go to a family, school, or community event, will someone make him/her feel embarrassed for being LGBTQ? If so, consider whether that's an environment where anyone in your immediate family needs to be.

    + Is there anyone your child feels is not safe or supportive? Ask your child for input on relationships that may be fraught or complicated and be willing to follow their lead.

6

"When Did You Decide to Be Gay?"

Greg

IF WE WERE GOING to commit to loving our son, Pastor Ed
had told us, we also needed to love his friends. In those early,
shell-shocked days, we didn't think much about that particular counsel. Of course we would welcome Greg Jr.'s friends.
That, at least, would be easy.

Lynn and I had always committed to providing an open
space for our kids' friends, because when we were dating, her
dad forbade her from seeing me, which just made us want to
pursue the relationship more. So, we were determined not to
cut off anyone who was important to our kids. No kid was
ever unwelcome in our house.

Throughout their childhood, we encouraged Connie and
Greg Jr. to bring friends home for dinner or sleepovers. It
helped that Lynn and I are both naturally drawn to people,
and we love to socialize. We loved having a full house. We'd
feed everyone and play board games with them. If we went to

the movies, we'd take a few of their friends with us. We'd bring them on family vacations. Over the years, it gave us many opportunities to observe how our kids treated others and how their peers treated them.

When kids are growing up, parents have a lot of control over who their friends are. If any of Greg Jr.'s high school friends were also gay, they knew better than to say it, and we'd never asked.

But when Greg Jr. moved to college, he set out to live an openly gay life, and many of his new friends were gay and lesbian. Few of them were Christians. Loving our son's friends, while still struggling to come to terms with his life, became a testing ground for us.

We still knew almost nothing about the LGBTQ community, other than it was something we wished wasn't part of our lives. When we tried to wade into the waters of our son's new life, we often lost our footing.

Lynn

I WORRIED ABOUT GREG Jr. living on his own. I still clung to the idea that we could protect him. But letting go and trusting God, I learned, is part of parenting. Every mom and dad faces it at some point, and it's tough on all of us.

Our job as parents is to "start children off in the way they should go" (Proverbs 22:6) and then to let them navigate the world on their own, fulfilling whatever God's unique purpose is for them. As writer Lori Freeland puts it: "While we don't pack our kids up and launch them full-speed ahead down the highway of life at eighteen, our relationship with them begins to change and transition between parent and child to parent and advisor and finally to parent and friend."*

I prayed for him every day, first, that God would show him his sin, and second, that he would be physically safe. Greg and I drove over to Chicago several times a year to visit Greg Jr. at DePaul. Whenever we were there, we would take him out for nice dinners and bring along anyone he wanted to invite. Greg Jr. and I also did a lot of shopping. He was studying fashion and interior design, and I loved to take him to his favorite stores and pick out things he liked. In other words, we showed our love for him in the ways we knew he enjoyed: spending time together, connecting over shared interests, and getting to know his friends.

From what I could see, Greg Jr. was a lot happier in the city than he'd been in Grand Rapids. He didn't tell us much about his life or what he was doing—and we didn't ask— but as always, we liked the friends that we met, both straight and gay.

Sure, we suspected that he was partying a lot, which worried us as parents. But we also had done our share of partying at his age, and overall, it looked like Greg Jr. had settled into a pretty good rhythm in the Windy City.

---

*Lori Freeland, "7 Ways to Survive Sending Your Child Off to College," *Crosswalk*, August 15, 2016, https://www.crosswalk.com/family/parenting/7-ways-to-survive -sending-your-child-off-to-college.html.

WHEN WE WITHDRAW FROM our children's lives, we end up sending a lot of mixed messages. We say that we love them, but our actions don't reflect it. We're no longer a safe place for them to bring the messy issues and questions they're dealing with. They withdraw, and the relationship becomes shallow.

Though Lynn and I made an effort to stay connected with Greg Jr., the relationship was strained, to say the least. Our conversations revolved around what some people call the "news, sports, and weather," which in our case was more like "food, fashion, and furniture." If it ever got deeper than that—like if Lynn started asking questions about Greg Jr.'s choices or what he believed—we'd all end up in a fight.

Years later, we found out just how much Greg Jr. kept from us. During the first quarter of his freshman year at DePaul, my son was the victim of a hate crime. This was one of the things I feared most when I found out that he was gay.

Greg Jr. wasn't doing anything dangerous when he was attacked. He was just visiting a female friend's apartment, but the boyfriend of the friend's roommate was also there, and after a few drinks, he started taunting Greg Jr. for being gay. Things escalated, and the roommate's boyfriend physically assaulted him. Greg Jr. fought back, things got bloody, and someone called the police.

When the officer asked if he wanted to press charges, Greg Jr. declined. He was afraid we'd find out, and he thought that if Lynn and I knew what had happened, we'd make him drop out of school and come back to Michigan. That, for him, was worse than being beaten.

Seventeen years later, the idea that someone threw my son to the ground and repeatedly kicked him just for being who he is still crushes my heart and makes my blood boil. But most of all, I'm devastated that Greg Jr. thought he couldn't tell us.

Lynn

DURING THOSE YEARS OF transition, Greg Jr. struggled under the pressure of our expectations. He kept his friends close to him whenever we visited, and almost always brought a few with him when he came home to Michigan. We didn't realize it then, but Greg Jr. later shared that he was using them as buffers against any awkward conversations or intrusive efforts we might try in his life.

What he saw as buffers, though, Greg and I saw as a mission field. The kids Greg Jr. brought home were bright, attractive, friendly young people, but most of them weren't walking with Jesus, and many of them were gay. So obviously we assumed that God had brought these young men and women into our home so that we could tell them what Jesus wanted them to know.

Greg and I love to cook, so we prepared great meals for them, played board games with them, and cleaned up after them. We came to love and care for many of Greg Jr.'s friends, but more than anything we wanted them to understand that Jesus loves the sinner but hates the sin.

I'm so embarrassed now to think about how many times I used that "love the sinner, hate the sin" cliché, and how deeply I believed it, even when it obviously didn't work.

Years before Greg Jr. told us he was gay, I was chatting on the phone with a good friend named Mimi, whom I'd known since I was a child. In the course of our conversation, she mentioned that her brother, someone I also knew, had come out as gay. I was shocked by the news. I remembered that Dan had often dated girls in high school, and I didn't think that he seemed like someone who would make what seemed like a terrible mistake in his life.

I reminded Mimi that God loved her brother, even if he hated what he'd chosen. "He loves the sinner, even if he hates the sin," I said with confidence.

Mimi was silent for a long moment. She didn't have a problem with her brother's sexual orientation, and my words clearly hurt her. When Mimi spoke again, she sounded angry. "You really don't get it, do you?"

"I do," I answered, and the Bible-preaching mama showed up. I explained that God's heart was broken by Dan's sexual sin, but he would never turn away from him completely. When he was ready to repent, I said, God would still be there.

The conversation didn't go well after that. Calling Dan a sinner was deeply offensive to Mimi. It sounded like I was saying that her brother's very existence was a sin, an offense against God. We argued for a while, and for the sake of our friendship we agreed to disagree.

Yet here I was, years later, still clinging to the same idea. I was sure that if I could just help my son's friends see that God was there, waiting for them to repent so that he could forgive them, their eyes would be opened. They would read the Bible and eventually thank me for showing them the way. And then they would help my son live a "normal" life, too.

Of course, that never happened. My words created walls rather than opened doors, because Greg Jr.'s friends didn't feel like they had anything to "repent" for. It was obvious that I saw them first as "sinners" instead of as human beings. Greg Jr.'s friends listened to me and didn't hear love; they heard hypocrisy, disdain, judgment, and me trying to fix them.

Greg

LYNN WASN'T ALONE IN thinking that the LGBTQ community was our new mission field. We both enjoyed getting to know the young people Greg Jr. brought into our lives, but we weren't subtle about trying to make them see the world the way we saw it.

I loved to take whoever was visiting out on our boat on sunny July afternoons. We'd throw the anchor out in one of Lake Michigan's beautiful bays and just float for a while. After some small talk, I would launch into a "casual" conversation about Jesus. I'd describe to them why we all needed Christ in our lives.

I remember one guy called me on it. "You're saying all of this because we're gay."

I denied it at the time. "No, let's take sex off the table. We all sin." I shared my own struggles. "I've wrestled with lying, lusting, gossiping, coveting, and more. At some point, we all fall short and we all hurt. We all need a savior."

That's what I believed, and still believe. But if I'm honest, I pushed my message harder with those young men than I would have with a group of straight coworkers or neighbors in the same situation, and I did it because they were gay. I was trying to fix something that I saw as broken, but these weren't engines in need of a tune-up; these were human beings who longed for genuine relationships and communication.

Lynn

THERE WAS ONE NIGHT I remember very clearly. Greg Jr. had brought a couple of friends with him for the weekend to our lake home in Harbor Springs. After dinner, while we all played board games at the table, I began to grill a sweet, outgoing guy named Scott about whether he was a Christian. Greg Jr. was mortified. "Mom, you've gotta stop," he kept saying.

But Scott wanted to talk. He told me he believed in God, and he believed in prayer. For example, not long ago he'd prayed that God would bring an ex-boyfriend back into his life, and God answered that prayer. The couple had reconciled.

I was horrified. "How do you know it wasn't Satan answering that prayer?" I asked him. "God wouldn't bring you into a homosexual relationship. That's *never* what God wants for you."

As if I had any idea what God wanted for a young man I'd just met.

Greg

I REMEMBER THAT NIGHT, too. Lynn was just tearing into this young man, and Greg Jr. was livid. He stormed away from the table, and I found him on the front porch, cooling off in the summer air.

"You've gotta get a handle on Mom," he told me, "or we're going back to Chicago tonight, and I'm not coming back." Greg Jr. had put up with a lot from us by then, but this was a breaking point. He'd had enough of the Bible-preaching mama.

Lynn and I talked, and she agreed to back off. She didn't want to chase her son or his friends away. I wasn't going to give up on the opportunity to help these young people see the error of their ways, though. I just tried a different approach.

My professional background is in sales and marketing, and I'd spent years looking for common ground with the people I met. It was natural for me to start conversations with a lot of questions, looking for common threads of understanding. When I showed a sincere interest in someone's life, I knew, people often opened up and shared their story.

To that end, one of the things I always asked gay men and women when I met them was "When did you decide to be gay?" It's hard to believe now, after multiple medical studies have shown that sexuality is at least partially hardwired from birth, but at the time it never occurred to me that the question was controversial. Like many evangelical Christians, I'd been told that being gay was a choice. I assumed that people who were gay believed that as well, and I thought asking about it was a way to get people to share their stories.

Not surprisingly, it didn't go as planned. No matter how many people I asked, I never met a single person who "decided" to be gay. Over and over, Greg Jr.'s friends patiently took the time to explain that they didn't choose this part of their identity. In fact, many of them responded with, "Are you crazy? Who would choose to be gay? Who would choose to be rejected by society, and become the focus of ridicule and the victim of hate crimes?"

What they said contradicted what I thought I knew. But these were the people who were living the experience. They were smart and outgoing, and they had a good point I'd never thought about. Why *would* they choose this?

I've been listening to the stories of gay men and women now for almost twenty years, and I've never met a single person who said they "decided" to be gay. Instead, most of them really struggled with their sexuality. People prayed that God would take their same-sex attraction away from them and grieved when it wasn't. Others hid their identity for a long time, fearing or knowing that they would be rejected by their family or church. And yet at the end of the day, those women and men are still who they have always been: people created in the image of God, who are still attracted to the same sex.

That realization, once it finally stuck with me, really changed the way I saw my son and our family. Until I was ready to admit that Greg Jr. was born gay, on some level I was always plagued with the idea that he could choose to be straight. And I wasn't alone in this. We've talked with hundreds of families who, when things get honest, confess their frustration. "Johnny made a bad decision in choosing to be gay, and bad decisions come with consequences. Johnny's bad decision is not only wrecking his life but is also destroying our family's good name and my reputation. If Johnny would just make a different decision, the right decision, none of us would be in this situation."

The more I looked into it, though, the more I understood that this attitude doesn't gel with the medical research. Study after study has uncovered new evidence that sexual orientation is based, at least in part, on genetic variations. In just one example, a 1993 study identified a region on the X chromosome in men that is linked to whether they are heterosexual or homosexual, and in 1995, a region on chromosome 8 was identified. Both findings were confirmed in a DNA study of gay and straight brothers in 2014.*

It was only when I understood that my child didn't choose to be gay any more than I signed up to be straight that I was ready to really come alongside him and support him through the difficult places. When I reached the point where I finally saw that long before my son was born God knew who Greg Jr. would be and whom he would love, I could finally see him as a full creation, wholly loved by God.

Years later, Lynn and I attended a panel discussion with six Christian adults who were lesbian, gay, or bisexual. The event was sponsored by our church in Atlanta for parents whose children identified as LGBTQ.

The moderator asked the panel a series of questions, but

---

*Andy Coghlan, "What Do the New 'Gay Genes' Tell Us About Sexual Orientation?" *New Scientist*, December 7, 2017, https://www.newscientist.com/article/2155810 -what-do-the-new-gay-genes-tell-us-about-sexual-orientation/.

two especially got my attention. The first question was this: "How many of you prayed to be made straight?"

Every one of them answered with a resounding "yes."

The second question was "If you could push a button today to be straight, would you push it?"

I was sure I knew what the answer would be. I was dead wrong.

Considering how much the panel had expressed that being LGBTQ was not something they chose, and they all shared how they had been deeply wounded by family members and their churches, I expected them all to jump for the imaginary button. Instead, they all said no. One person said, "I'm not entirely sure I'd be a Christian if I wasn't gay. Being gay forced me to really examine my faith." Another agreed, adding, "Nothing forces you to examine your faith like having everyone tell you 'You're not a Christian, God hates you, and you're going to hell.'"

Parents as well report that even if they originally prayed for God to "fix" their child and make them straight, over time they discover that this journey has deepened their faith and brought them closer to Jesus in ways they'd never imagined.

Lynn

I'D PROMISED GREG JR. that I would tone down my "Bible-preaching mama" voice, but I still looked for chances to talk to my son's friends about Jesus.

One morning I remember as being very special. Greg Jr. was visiting, and he'd brought home a friend named Justin. I immediately thought Justin was a sweet guy, outgoing and easy to talk to. He was a few years older than Greg Jr. and they acted like brothers, with Justin always looking out for my son. Of course, I immediately loved him for that. As the weekend progressed, though, I thought there was also something sad about him.

I got up early and made a pot of coffee. As I was pouring my first cup, Justin came into the kitchen. I poured him a cup too, and the two of us sat comfortably in the family room and chatted. I asked him all kinds of questions, and he answered them easily. We talked about growing up in Kansas, and about his siblings and his parents. I found out that he had a turbulent relationship with his dad but was close to his mom. Maybe that's why he trusted me.

Justin was the first person to really open up and tell me what it was like to be a young gay man in Chicago. He told me how hard it had been to come out and what he worried about now.

And for once, maybe for the first time, I remember that I just listened. I didn't interrupt, I didn't try to lead the conversation to some spiritual outcome. I just entered into this young man's life and met him as a fellow creation—loved, sinful, hopeful, and made in the image of God.

Listening, I realized, was a powerful parenting tool that I hadn't been paying nearly enough attention to.

ONE OF THE THINGS I love about being a follower of Jesus is that he is filled with grace toward people like me, who are often oblivious to the obvious.

In the fall of 1985, just a week after Lynn and I made the decision to follow Jesus, we stumbled into a small, conservative church near our home. After the service was over, the young pastor, a man named Brian, stood at the back of the sanctuary and greeted everyone as they left.

When Lynn and I reached the front of the line, I shook his hand heartily and introduced myself, adding, "Hey, that was one hell of a sermon!"

Now, remember that I was brand new in my faith and fairly un-churched. I was oblivious to what was obvious to everyone else: that people in church talked differently than what I was used to at work and in my neighborhood.

What made all the difference, though, was how Pastor Brian responded. He roared with laughter, even as everyone else looked at me with raised eyebrows. He didn't judge me or make me feel awkward or unwanted. Instead Brian and his wife, Judy, befriended Lynn and me and invested heavily in discipling us over the better part of the next year. To this day we remain fabulous friends.

Over and over during those years, Lynn and I experienced the same kind of grace from my son and his friends. When we were oblivious to the obvious, they were patient. When we said all the wrong things, they opened their lives and showed us their humanity.

Back at the beginning of our journey, Pastor Ed had told us "The gay community has been terribly mistreated, and in some ways, they have become the lepers of our society today." The deeper into our journey we got, the more we saw the truth of this.

I wish I could say the same for the rest of the people around us.

One summer, Greg Jr. brought half a dozen of his friends to stay with us at the lake. For most of their visit, we were either in our house or out on the boat, but one night, Lynn and I took the whole group into town for dinner.

We were in a small, often sleepy-feeling town, and I noticed that our table of young, happy men enjoying themselves was drawing the attention of many patrons in the restaurant. Some of them, judging from their expressions, didn't approve.

Early the next morning, Lynn and I went for a run. As we wove through town, we came across graffiti on the sidewalk that said:

No gays allowed.

Gays go home.

I was furious. As a straight, white, successful midwestern man, I'd never been the victim of slurs or hate speech. And until that day, I'd never had to put myself in the position of someone who was a minority in a culture that treated them with suspicion and outright hatred. Yet this, I realized, was my son's experience every day.

Sure, maybe it was just one or a handful of kids who defaced the sidewalk. But to me, this town that was known for being "family friendly" had made a cowardly attack on my

family and our guests, and the worst part was that there was
nothing I could do about it.

Lynn

BIT BY BIT, GOD shook our foundations. We'd gotten past the
initial, life-stopping fear, but we were nowhere near embracing our new lives. I was still desperately asking God to show
me a way out of this, still praying for the strength to persevere
through the darkness around me.

For the first few years after Greg Jr. came out, my Bible
reading centered around what I thought God wanted me to
tell my son. Over and over, I'd read the "clobber verses"—the
not-so-gentle name that has evolved for the six passages of
Scripture that seem to address same-sex relationships and ac-
tivities. But over time, I started to ask questions about the rest
of Scripture. *What else did Jesus say that might help me in my
current dilemma?*

Greg and I had Bibles that printed all the words spoken
directly by Jesus in red, and we started to explore those red
letters. What did Jesus, the Savior of the world and the Lord
of my heart, tell people like me? How did he convert sinners?
How did he engage in relationships? Who did he hang out
with, and how did he treat the people he encountered?

What was I missing?

That was the question I was asking when I came across
Jesus' parable of the Good Samaritan in Luke 10. Of course,
after two decades in church I already knew the story about

the Jewish man who traveled alone on a dusty road. I knew about the robbers who beat him and left him naked and half-dead. I knew about the two respected Jewish leaders who walked by without stopping to help. And I knew about the Samaritan, the stranger from a disrespected place, who saw the man and "took pity on him."

When I read the story this time, though, I saw something different. Instead of focusing on the righteous Samaritan man who gave his time and money to someone less fortunate, I paid attention to the religious leaders.

The priest and the Levite were the ones who were *supposed* to know right from wrong, and yet they walked to the other side of the road and left the wounded man to die alone—all because their religious rules didn't permit them to touch someone "unclean." But a Samaritan, a man who had been ostracized by almost everyone, saw a human being who needed help and he gave up everything: his own safety, his time, his comfort, his money, his ride, and even his reputation. What would his neighbors think to see him serving their enemy? To see him spending money at a Jewish inn? It didn't matter. He was fine being misunderstood.

The Samaritan man did what was right by showing love to his neighbor—another human—rather than adhering to and strictly following his religious rules. This was a real-life example that I could suddenly understand as I started to establish real relationships with a modern group of outcasts.

THE GOOD SAMARITAN'S STORY, and the new way God was showing us to understand it, reminded me of something else I'd once read.

Back in the 1990s, the evangelist Billy Graham was invited to attend an event for then president Bill Clinton. Reverend Graham had been a nonpartisan "pastor of presidents" since Harry Truman's administration, but this event was controversial. It was scheduled not long after President Clinton admitted to having a sexual affair, and there were plenty of Christians, especially in conservative church circles, who complained about Reverend Graham agreeing to appear with the president.

As he arrived at the event, a reporter asked Reverend Graham, "Why are you here supporting this man after everything he has done to this country?"

Reverend Graham's response made a lasting impression on me. He said, "It is the Holy Spirit's job to convict, God's job to judge, and my job to love."

Wow.

Pastor Ed had told us to love our son and love his friends. But instead of showing love, I'd been trying to take the Holy Spirit's job of convicting my son and his friends. I thought it was up to me to show them how their behavior, and their very identity, didn't match what I thought it should be. And when they didn't change, I took on God's role of judgment, too.

Looking back, I can see that Lynn and I were struggling

through this season not because we had a gay son, but because *we didn't trust God with our son.* God patiently showed us time after time that our job was to love, and yet we kept trying to grab the reins. When I thought, *We need to convict them* and *We need to judge them,* I was really saying, "I don't think you've got this under control, God. I think we need to step in and do your work for you."

Parenting a child is one of the biggest testers of faith that a person will ever face. Until a parent can say to God, "My child is yours, and we trust you," our experiences with our child will be strained. Our relationship with God will be strained. And our lives will lack the fullness and joy that God wants us to have.

Key Learnings: Make It Personal

+ Welcoming your child's LGBTQ friends may be an uncomfortable experience for you, especially if you aren't used to interacting with your kids' friends. During this season of transition, though, make an extra effort to show love to the people your child cares about. You're on a steep learning curve, and engaging with your child's community will help you understand them in a deeper, more personal way. Invite your child to bring friends over for dinner or holiday gatherings, or join them at events. Visit them where they live as much as possible so that you can engage with their world.

✦ Shower your child and their friends with love, but remember that it's not your job to save or fix them. This is not a time to get into a debate about what Scripture says about sexuality or to try to witness to someone, and debating the Bible almost always ends disastrously. Instead, focus on showing love for each person wherever they are and focus on building trust and a relationship. If God wants you to speak into someone's life, he'll bring you both to the conversation naturally.

✦ When your child leaves home, don't ask too many questions about things you're not ready to hear. When they were younger, it was your job to protect them, encourage them in their walk with the Lord, and care for their needs. But now it's time to let go and trust God. Pray for them every day—even several times a day—but don't dwell too much on what they're doing.

✦ The pressure of being part of an often misunderstood and marginalized group puts your LGBTQ child at a higher risk for depression and harmful behavior including drugs, promiscuous sex, and self-harm. Pay attention to your child's moods and watch for physical or emotional withdrawal, dramatic shifts in mood or actions, or feelings of hopelessness. If you see any of these behaviors, encourage your child to seek professional counseling to help them adjust.

+ Listen more than you talk. Many people who are
  LGBTQ expect, sadly, to be condemned and judged
  by Christians and the church. Their stories are often
  full of rejection and pain. Give them a reason to see
  Jesus' followers as people who are genuinely inter-
  ested in them as human beings equally created and
  loved by God. Ask where a person grew up, whether
  they have siblings, what they like to study if they're in
  school, and what they like to do for fun. Engage with
  their hearts and minds, not just the label that defines
  part of who they are.

7

"He's My Boyfriend"

Lynn

THIS WAS A SEASON of perseverance and of pressing forward, even if we didn't understand why God had brought us here. The shock of having a gay son was wearing off, and we were learning to interact with Greg Jr. for who he was, not who we wanted him to be.

But there were still things we didn't—couldn't—talk about, like romantic relationships.

When it came to our kids, there was a definite double standard in how we handled Greg Jr.'s love life and Connie's. No matter how much we wanted to be part of our kids' lives, I can't remember a single time that we asked Greg Jr. if he was seeing anyone special or suggested that we would want to meet someone he dated.

Partly that's because of how our children communicate. Connie has always been more open with her life. When she was a kid, we joked she couldn't keep a secret. Now that she's a wife and mother herself, we know she doesn't tell us every-thing, but she's still very connected to our day-to-day lives.

Greg Jr. kept things more to himself. Maybe it's because he's a son and not a daughter, or maybe it's because he had held the secret of his orientation for so many years that he got used to keeping things to himself. Or maybe it's just because people are different, and we each communicate in different ways.

The real reason for our double standard was the simple fact that Greg and I were more comfortable with the idea of Connie dating, marrying, and building a family than we were with Greg Jr. doing the same. For us, and for many parents, knowing that our child is LGBTQ is one thing, but seeing it can really shine a spotlight on the elephant in the room.

I knew in theory that Greg Jr. was dating. He was a young, active, attractive, social man, and he'd told us in no uncertain terms that he wouldn't be celibate and that one day he would like to find someone to share his life with. But he never brought boyfriends home, and I never asked about it.

It's not that he locked us out, but I didn't know what I didn't know. And for a long time, like many parents, I didn't want to know. I wasn't ready to interact with him as a part of a couple.

At least, I wasn't ready to interact with him in a relation-ship with another man. I confess that for far too long I held out hope that my gay son would fall in love with a woman. In the five stages of grief first laid out by Elisabeth Kübler-Ross, this is considered denial, and lots of parents get stuck here: *"You just haven't found the right [opposite sex] person yet. Even-*

tually you'll want to find a traditional partner, settle down, and have a 'normal' family."

When Greg was in college, one of his best friends was a beautiful straight girl named Annie. She would come to our house on school breaks, and we'd see her when we went to Chicago. Annie was around so much that when Greg and I took the kids on a spring break vacation to the beach, it seemed perfectly natural to invite her to come along with us. At least, that's what I told Greg Jr. In the back of my mind I thought that this would be a chance for them to realize they were in love (which of course didn't happen).

Mostly, Greg Jr. just rolled his eyes and ignored my fantasies. He was busy developing his own thoughts and dreams for the future. Once, when I mentioned to him that I sometimes still wished I could be a grandmother to his children, his quick comeback was "What makes you think I'm not having children?"

Oh, I thought, *what does that look like? Here's another chapter I'm not ready for.* Michigan had only recently made adoption legal for LGBTQ couples, and the practice was controversial. Gay marriage was still a long way away. It was hard to imagine my gay son with a family of his own.

Greg

FOR PARENTS OF CHILDREN who are gay and lesbian, this question about relationships is often emotionally charged, especially considering how much the culture has changed in the course of our lifetime. When we grew up, it was almost unheard of for a gay or lesbian couple to publicly acknowledge their relationship. Our kids, on the other hand, are used to seeing LGBTQ couples move through familiar paths of dating, marriage, and parenting.

I remember the first dad who came to me with concerns about his son's wedding. William really struggled with his son's identity as a gay adult, and their relationship had been fragile for years. Now the "save the date" card sent him and his wife, Laura, into a spiral of despair. Would their presence at the wedding "condone" their son's relationship? Would not attending break the relationship for good?

The family was divided about whether they could, in good conscience, attend the ceremony. Over lunch one day, I listened to William weigh his options and consider all the things that could go wrong. He was worried about offending his mother and mother-in-law. One said she would never attend the wedding, and the other was offended that they even had the conversation, because of course she would go. He was worried about what people would think. He was worried about what God would think.

At some point, he asked what I would do. Though Lynn and I hadn't personally faced the question ourselves, we'd been through a few things that gave me a context for how to answer him, starting with Greg Jr.'s first boyfriend.

Our family lived in that "don't ask, don't tell" place for a long time, but eventually something happened that Greg Jr. couldn't keep from us.

He had his heart broken.

After a few years at DePaul, Greg Jr. moved to New York City to attend FIT, the Fashion Institute of Technology. He seemed happy at first. He was studying something he loved and had made good friends in the Big Apple.

But then early one morning, as Lynn and I were just waking up, I noticed an email from Greg Jr. marked "Urgent." I remember thinking, *That's never a good sign.*

Our son had written at four in the morning, and he sounded upset. He had caught his boyfriend cheating on him, and in the fight that followed they'd broken up. Greg Jr. was devastated, and his email said he couldn't stay in the city anymore. He wanted to come home.

I handed my phone to Lynn so that she could read the message while I thought about what to do next. We hadn't even known that Greg Jr. was seeing someone, and now we were in the middle of a breakup. *How should we handle this? How serious had Greg Jr. been with this guy?*

Lynn

I WAS STILL READING the email when our land line rang. It was Greg Jr., deeply hurt and upset by the betrayal he'd experienced.

Greg and I each picked up an extension, and we tried to console our vulnerable son. Greg told him how sorry we were that he had to go through this.

"Maybe your friend will change his mind," I added.

There was a long silence on the other end of the line.

"He's not my *friend*, Mom. He's my boyfriend. Don't. Call. Him. My. Friend."

I apologized and said that he knew what I meant, and the conversation continued. But then I did it again. I referred to him as Greg Jr.'s *friend*.

That sent the conversation seriously downhill. "I can't take this right now," he snapped. "I'm getting off the phone." And then he hung up.

I sat back, feeling defensive. *What was his problem?* I hadn't said anything wrong. He was just feeling sensitive right now.

But then, slowly, I heard God whispering to my heart. If it was Connie calling before dawn to grieve a breakup, would I have said the same thing? Did I ever hesitate to refer to her partners as boyfriends or to imagine her giving her heart to someone?

I sat and tried to really picture Greg Jr. in a relationship with a partner whom he loved. I couldn't do it. I had to call this person who broke my son's heart his friend because I subconsciously couldn't think about my son giving his heart to another guy.

I had a new question to add to my prayer list. *God, how do I handle my son's need for companionship? How do I react when he falls in love?*

Greg

GREG JR. LEFT NEW York City not long after that phone call. He came back to Michigan for a while, and then went back to

Chicago to finish his degree at DePaul. He was approaching his midtwenties by then.

At his age, I had been married, had a family, and owned a business, yet in many ways Lynn and I still parented our son as if he were a teenager. When Greg Jr. brought friends home with him for vacations and holidays, we insisted that everyone sleep in separate beds, even those whom we knew were dating. The Bible's standards about extramarital sex were clear to us, we explained, and there were things we just weren't going to allow under our roof.

But then our niece and her boyfriend came to visit for a weekend. We knew they were living together but were not married. After some discussion about whether we should try to enforce the appearance of chastity where we knew none existed, Lynn and I decided to let them choose their own sleeping arrangements. We reasoned that it wasn't up to us to dictate the behavior of others. We had been their age once, and not sharing a room hadn't kept us from doing whatever we wanted. The young couple, not surprisingly, chose to share a single room, and we didn't say a word.

Sometime later, two friends our own age visited. They were both recently divorced from other people and were dating each other. Now, Jesus has some pretty tough words about divorce and remarriage, but again, Lynn and I decided we weren't comfortable enforcing a "separate beds" policy with our peers.

What had been a small, nagging concern in my mind every time Greg Jr. visited became much bigger as the truth became harder to avoid. We were treating our son and his friends differently than the straight couples who visited us. If our niece's and our friends' behavior was between them and God, why was Greg Jr.'s any different? My actions, I realized, reeked of hypocrisy.

Lynn

BY THIS POINT, GREG and I were swimming in the deep end of the pool, theologically speaking. We spent long hours studying the Bible, desperately seeking to learn more about Jesus' character and how we should live, and especially how we should live in community with the people around us.

We'd learned that our job wasn't to judge or to change the people he brought into our lives. But it still seemed uncomfortable to live among the things that our church community had condemned for so long. Once again, we turned to the red letters.

How did Jesus treat those who lived differently than him? The Bible doesn't record any story of Jesus interacting with a person who was gay, and he never talks about homosexuality directly. But we knew he spent plenty of time with people who, like today's LGBTQ community, were considered outsiders (or worse) by the religious establishment.

In first-century Galilee, the "outsiders" included Samaritans, tax collectors, prostitutes, and women in general. The religious leaders of the day shunned those people and encouraged their followers to do so as well. It was, for them, a question of obeying what God said in the Torah. They believed

that setting themselves apart as followers of God meant punishing those who lived outside his laws.

That's why Jesus' behavior drove the Pharisees and other
religious leaders crazy. The more we read, the more we realized that when Jesus met outsiders, he engaged them. He
spent time with them. He blessed them. He never shunned or
looked at anyone with disgust.

"I desire mercy, not sacrifice," he says in Matthew 9, quot-
ing the prophet Hosea.

During the Sermon on the Mount, he directly contradicted the religious traditions of separation when he said,
"You have heard that it was said, 'Love your neighbor and
hate your enemy.' But I tell you, love your enemies and pray
for those who persecute you."

And then in Luke 6: "If you love those who love you, what
credit is that to you? . . . But love your enemies, do good to them,
and lend to them without expecting to get anything back."

The more Greg and I focused on who Jesus was, the more
we couldn't miss his gentle, tender, and loving spirit. Time
after time, he chose those with the greatest needs. He didn't
talk down to the outsiders. He treated all people as equals,
just as they were.

Greg

JESUS' BEHAVIOR WAS NOTHING short of radical in his day. I
kept coming back to the story of Jesus' conversation with the
Pharisees in John 8:

At dawn he appeared again in the temple courts, where all the people gathered around him, and he sat down to teach them. The teachers of the law and the Pharisees brought in a woman caught in adultery. They made her stand before the group and said to Jesus, "Teacher, this woman was caught in the act of adultery. In the Law Moses commanded us to stone such women. Now what do you say?"

John says that *they were using this question as a trap, in order to have a basis for accusing him.* Jesus had been traveling around the country, preaching his message of grace and acceptance. He healed a lame man on the Sabbath, which infuriated those who claimed that was working on the day God set aside for rest. The carpenter from Nazareth was breaking the laws that God had established.

The religious leaders found a new way to publicly test Jesus' commitment to the authority of Scripture. "Now what do you say?" they asked, and then waited for him to say the wrong thing.

The leaders clearly weren't asking Jesus for permission to carry out the woman's punishment, because the Law of Moses already gave them that. There wasn't much wiggle room when it came to what to do with an adulterer. What the Pharisees wanted to know—and what they wanted everyone around them to hear—was whether Jesus would side with the Torah and obey what was written or continue on with his crazy ministry of grace.

The gospel of John tells us that Jesus bent down and

started to write on the ground. We don't know what he wrote or whether it had any impact on what happened next. What we do know is that Jesus finally stood and said only, "Let any of you who is without sin be the first to throw a stone at her."

Centuries later, we've turned that same idea into the lesson "Those who live in glass houses shouldn't throw stones."

I can just imagine how silent it got. This group of powerful men had set out to shame someone who they clearly thought was beneath them, but now the tables were turned.

The text says eventually, some of the oldest men in the group walked away. The book of John doesn't tell us why, but we assume that regardless of what the Torah said about how this woman should be stoned, the scholars acknowledged they were not worthy to be its enforcers.

One by one, the others followed, until Jesus was the only one left with the woman.

"Woman, where are they? Has no one condemned you?"

"No one, sir," she said.

"Then neither do I condemn you," Jesus declared.

"Go now and leave your life of sin."

I have friends who also study the Bible carefully, and they like to point out Jesus' last words: "Go now and leave your life of sin."

But did she sin again? The Bible doesn't tell us, because Jesus didn't hold back his grace until she acted in the way he wanted her to. He didn't say, "Leave your life of sin, *and then* I won't condemn you." No, he accepted her right where she was, in the middle of whatever mess her life was in. He explained that he wouldn't judge her first, and then he offered his thoughts on how she could have a better future.

Lynn

I LOVE THAT STORY and how Jesus stands in solidarity with the woman who was dragged to the temple courts. (Ever wonder where her partner in adultery was in all of this, by the way? Why did the Pharisees bring only one person to Jesus?)

Because Jesus was sinless, he alone could have condemned her for her actions, but instead he showed only grace. Time after time, we found Bible passages that confirmed that Jesus loved people right where they were, for who they were. Even if his culture condemned them, he loved them.

It was hard not to draw comparisons to how Greg and I had been responding to the people and behaviors that our culture condemned.

Greg

FOR YEARS WE'D BEEN trying to walk the fine line of loving Greg Jr. but also making it clear to everyone we knew that we didn't condone his behavior. Being seen as good Christians was more important to us than how we treated one another.

Our reputation was more important than our family. And that, we realized, wasn't what God wanted.

As another parent of an LGBTQ child said, "I want to be more concerned about my child's first name than my last name."

When Lynn and I were confronted with the truth of our motivations and the lessons from Jesus' example, we dropped our "who sleeps where" restrictions, and just in time.*

Because Greg Jr. fell in love again, and this time he invited us to meet the guy.

Greg Jr. was twenty-six, out of school, and building a career in Chicago. Lynn and I were planning a visit to him for a weekend when he said, too casually, "There's someone I'd like you to meet while you're here."

Greg Jr. had a boyfriend, Jon, and they were serious enough that he wanted to introduce us. This, obviously, was a first.

Lynn and I said of course we'd like to meet him.

Lynn

I WAS CURIOUS ABOUT what kind of person Jon would be, and how Greg Jr. would act with him. I wondered how all four of us would get along. First impressions are important and can

---

*This doesn't mean that we encourage other families to adopt an "open bedroom" policy. It's a tough question, with good arguments to be made on both sides. Every family should prayerfully come to their own conclusion. What God convicted us about was the hypocrisy of the double standard we were creating.

make or break a relationship before it ever forms. We wanted to know more about this person, especially how he treated our son and where he was spiritually.

There was a lot of potential for awkwardness, given our history of making Greg Jr.'s friends into projects. But Greg and I were trying to love our son differently now, and so we agreed that we would approach this meeting with the same open hearts as if Connie was introducing us to a boyfriend.

In the end, it all went very well. The four of us had a nice dinner. Jon was clearly nervous, and it was clear to me that Greg Jr. had carefully prepped him about what he should and shouldn't say to us. But Jon was also very bright, very social, and a pleasure to be with. As we watched him interact with our son, we could see that there was an easy connection between them. They enjoyed each other's company, and they were clearly each other's best friend. That was good to see.

As we walked out of the restaurant together, laughing and talking, it struck me: It had been almost ten years since we first found out that our son was attracted to men. Back then, I never would have imagined that God would bring us to this place.

Greg

I THOUGHT ABOUT ALL of that years later, when William asked me what I thought he should do about his son's wedding. A decade before, I would have recoiled at the thought of attending a same-sex wedding. But now, God led me to not answer directly, at first, but to change the subject a little.

Over the years, I said, Lynn and I had attended dozens of weddings. Sometimes we knew the couple very well, sometimes we only knew either the bride or the groom, and sometimes we only knew the parents. More than a few couples in those weddings had been living together for years before they tied the knot. And though Lynn and I believe that God created sex to be enjoyed only within the boundaries of marriage, we never avoided a wedding because of the couple's previous sex life. We never felt like our presence was somehow putting a "Christian stamp of approval" on their choices.

Knowing that about ourselves, Lynn and I would attend the same-sex weddings of our friends, and perhaps someday of our son, as a way of loving them and maintaining a presence and influence in their lives. I explained to William that we would be following in the footsteps of Jesus, who never hesitated to share a meal or a celebration with anyone, regardless of how they lived their day-to-day lives.

Key Learnings: Make It Personal

+ If you are the parent of a child who is LGBTQ, at some point you will be faced with the question of how to address your child's attraction to another person. Don't avoid it (or them). Be ready to talk openly about the realities of being sexually active for anyone outside marriage. Let them know you love them, and that you're concerned that being sexually active will put your child at a higher risk for sexually transmitted diseases.* If they're willing to talk with you about it, discuss how they will safeguard themselves physically, emotionally, and spiritually.

✦ Once you've had the initial conversation about safety and responsible behavior, the best advice we have is to stop thinking about the sex. For many parents, this is a sticky point. We struggle to get past mental pictures of a physical relationship that is outside what we have known or experienced. But most of us rarely think about the sex lives of the straight people we meet. Apply that same standard. Focus on the many other things that make your child a unique creation of God.

✦ When your child enters a relationship, meet their new love interest as soon as your child invites you to. This man or woman who has caught your child's attention is incredibly important to them, and you will build a deeper relationship by showing you genuinely care.

✦ If possible, engage with your LGBTQ child's boyfriend or girlfriend in the same way you would if their straight sibling brought home a significant other. Ask about their dreams, aspirations, and spiritual life. Ask how you can pray for them. Observe what this person sees and loves in your child. Creating a welcoming, warm, fun environment is a sign of your love for your

---

*This is a genuine concern backed up by the Circle Care Center: http://circlecarecenter .org/popular-stories/same-sex-relationships-and-stds.

child, and it opens a door for you to continue to have a place of influence in your child's life.

+ Guard yourself against the hypocrisy of a double standard, and prayerfully consider how Jesus would interact with any person, gay or straight, who has different values, beliefs, or orientations. Seek ways to consistently offer love to everyone.

8

Let's Talk About Surviving

Psychologists say that the human mind cannot stay in a place of paralyzing fear and denial forever. Eventually, a person's survival instinct kicks in, and the mind starts to adapt to a new normal and to seek ways to live in that space.

Discovering that our child was LGBTQ was a twist in our life story that we didn't seek, and to be honest, one that we didn't particularly want. But once we realized that we didn't have a choice—Greg Jr. couldn't just be quickly and quietly "fixed," and we couldn't stay isolated in our closet of fear forever—we had to start finding a new way to live with our new normal.

In other words, we had to learn how to *survive*.

If you'd talked to us during those tumultuous early years after Greg Jr. came out, we would have told you, "We don't understand what's happening or why, but we're pressing through it." Being the parents of an LGBTQ child felt like something we needed to *endure*, maybe a test God was giving us to see how we would serve him. We certainly didn't see it as a place where we could ever discover joy.

While the specific path differs for every family, in our experience most Christian parents of LGBTQ children go through a season where the best they can do is focus on surviving. It's a long, bumpy, complicated time, full of conflicting emotions, false starts, spiritual battles, and conflict in relationships. But the good news is that there is a reason for this season, and the struggles we face here are what ultimately lead us to stronger characters and life-changing discoveries about God's deepest desires for us.

Only after we learned to trust God with our family and our relationships did we understand that the dreams we once had for ourselves paled in comparison to what he had in store for us.

What Do We Mean When We Talk About Surviving?

WHEN WE TALK ABOUT a person who is focused on surviving, we're referring to those who live despite an underlying sense of loss. They're past the place of fear. They've gotten over the anger. Things for them are actually a lot better than they were in the crisis stage. The tears have passed. Now, the word that they use most often to describe their attitude is "tired." Surviving takes a lot of energy.

Fear, as we've seen, can leave us paralyzed and unable to process what's happening around us. People who are focused on surviving, on the other hand, have usually made a conscious decision to become active in their own situations . . . but that action can be sporadic and inconsistent.

During our long years of surviving as Greg Jr.'s parents, we tried to be active in a lot of ways. We tried to "love the sinner but hate the sin." We shared Bible verses with people who didn't ask for them. We ignored or avoided important parts of our son's life. We engaged for the first time with others in the LGBTQ community, but we made them into mission projects. We fiercely defended our son against any outside force, even as we withdrew ourselves and alienated him with our disapproval.

In hindsight, it's clear that we were flailing, looking for something solid to hold on to and to give us direction in a world that had shifted radically under our feet.

There must be something we can do to get us out of this uncomfortable place. This must be some kind of test. What can we do to make this better?

We looked for answers, but often in the wrong places. And in this, we weren't alone.

Christian parents of LGBTQ children mostly enter this surviving stage with a commitment to protect their family, even as they quietly (or not so quietly) wish that that part of their child's identity didn't exist. We love our children, and we want to be part of their lives, but if we're honest, we don't want *this* part of their story. We try to be safe harbors, even as that brings us to places our churches told us were never safe.

We're thrust into a culture war we never chose, and parenting starts to feel like a thorn that God inexplicably gave us to endure. Or perhaps it's a problem that God needs us to solve.

We don't understand what God is doing—and sometimes we secretly wonder if he's doing anything at all.

Perseverance

MANY OF THE FAMILIES we meet and minister to are committed to preserving appearances, regardless of whether their hearts are in their relationships or not. They can't imagine living with joy, but they're determined to *persevere*. When they're honest, they admit, "This is the challenge that God has trusted me with. He may have called me to suffer in ways that most parents don't have to, but I'll press forward and make the best of it."

Perseverance is not a bad thing. It demonstrates discipline and a commitment to continue over the long haul even in the face of difficulty. The parents who persevere in their relationship with their children, despite their own discomfort, demonstrate love for their families. Christians who persevere in seeking God's will in Scripture and community, despite feeling like they're being judged, demonstrate their love for God.

But perseverance alone does not reflect everything that God desires for us. Our Father loves us, and he wants us to experience lives that are more than just battles of endurance. He wants us to find joy in what he gives us. He wants us to engage deeply with others as fellow creations. And most of all, he wants us to share life with him and with one another, and we can't do that when we're spending all our energy trying to get past this "detour" in life.

People who are focused only on perseverance can become distracted by their own discomfort and start to believe that it's up to them—using their own efforts and strength—to change what they want to see changed.

The Desire for Control

FOR US, THE BIGGEST, hardest thing about the period of surviving our new roles as the parents of a gay son was learning, over and over again, that we weren't in control.

Our psychologist and pastor friends remind us often that human beings, when reacting to feelings of helplessness and vulnerability, often try to fix the situation by regaining control over some part of it. They think there's something they can do to make their situation better. They assume that God needs *them* to redeem the situation that he created.

That sense that "God made a mistake when he created our LGBTQ children, and it's up to us to fix it" leaves parents always on guard. When we think that we're in control of our lives and our families, we tend to stop asking God what he wants, and we stop listening to his gentle directions.

Instead of resting in God's plan, we start making our own. We'll get people saved! We'll enforce rules! We'll show everyone the error of their ways! We will change people!

No wonder the season of surviving is so exhausting.

Of course, trying to control the future never works. In Paul's second letter to the Corinthians, he reminds us that the real way to escape trials and challenges is exactly the opposite: instead of taking control, we need to give even more to God:

"We were crushed and overwhelmed beyond our ability to endure, and we thought we would never live through it. In fact, we expected to die. But as a result, we stopped relying on ourselves and learned to rely only on God, who raises the dead" (2 Corinthians 1:8b–9 NLT).

What Does God Say About Surviving?

GOD ACKNOWLEDGES THAT THERE'S a place for perseverance in the journey. When things are painful, or when we're suffering, God develops our character through our perseverance. Over and over, we see where Jesus persevered through suffering, discouragement, and unjust criticism. We're in good company.

But at the same time, perseverance is not the place where he wants us to stay. It's something for us to pass through on the way to the ultimate goal, which is hope.

Over and over, the New Testament promises us a future filled with grace and hope: "Being confident of this, that he who began a good work in you will carry it on to completion until the day of Christ Jesus" (Philemon 1:6).

Satan wants to rob us of that. He wants to break our families apart, to kill our relationships with one another, and to trick us into thinking that God can't handle the difficult corners of our lives. He tries to convince us that what's happening is all an accident. But Scripture says that no one, and nothing, is an accident.

Our Heavenly Father made each person in the world in his image. "For you created my inmost being; you knit me together in my mother's womb. I praise you because I am fearfully and wonderfully made; your works are wonderful, I know that full well. My frame was not hidden from you when I was made in the secret place, when I was woven together in the depths of the earth. *Your eyes saw my unformed body; all the days ordained for me were written in your book before one of them came to be*" (Psalm 139:13–16, emphasis added).

God knew, long before we did, that we would be in this place. This place includes our LGBTQ children, their non-Christian friends, the people in the church who are quick to judge them, and the people in the world who might try to hurt them. And he has a purpose for us being here. His ultimate plan is not for us to stay in places where we suffer. His goal is for us to live full, abundant, and joy-filled lives.

"The thief does not come except to steal, and to kill and to destroy. I have come that they may have life and that they may have it more abundantly" (John 10:10).

But getting to that place of abundance requires time, humility, and a whole lot of trust.

What Does It Take to Get Past Survival?

ON THE SURFACE, SURVIVAL doesn't look much like fear. It's active, driven even.

Yet underneath, there's a common theme: both are about pride. When we're caught up in the perseverance of surviving, we're still relying on ourselves—our own efforts, our own answers, our own strength—to navigate the unexpected places where God brings us.

We still haven't really reached the place of trusting him.

The journey toward a life of abundance starts with re-committing ourselves to the fundamental knowledge that God is in control of everything, and then continues through constant reminders that we can trust him with even the painful parts of our lives. This happens, most often, in baby steps. A meaningful verse of Scripture or conversation opens our hearts to a new idea, and we move ahead. Sometimes, we slip back into old habits and thoughtless actions, but often, the truth sticks, and we change. Gradually, if we are committed to letting God take control, things change, and a new perspective emerges.

When author Lysa TerKeurst visited Michelangelo's famous sculpture of David in Florence, she was struck by a quote from the artist. When someone asked how he made the statue, he said, "I saw the angel in the marble and carved until I set him free."

Lysa's prayer that day was "O God, chisel me. I don't want to be locked in my hard perceptions forever. I want to be all that You have in mind for me to be."*

God will do that for us, if we ask. He will use the sharp points of events we never thought we wanted in our lives to chip away the rough parts of our characters, bringing us from fear to surviving, and then from surviving to hope.

---

*Lysa TerKeurst, "Called to Freedom," Encouragement for Today, February 8, 2018, https://www.crosswalk.com/devotionals/encouragement/encouragement-for-today-february-8-2018.html.

But to get there, we must trust the Master Artist. We must accept that God created our children for a reason, and he knows "all the days ordained" for them, including the difficult ones. It's not our job to understand the reason or to bend it to our will. All we can do is accept that his "works are wonderful." Nothing is too big for him, and nothing surprises him.

Psalm 62:8 reminds us that we can "trust in him at all times, you people; pour out your hearts to him, for God is our refuge." And a few dozen chapters later, the psalmist reminds us that God is all-knowing and all powerful: "He determines the number of the stars and calls them each by name. Great is our Lord and mighty in power; his understanding has no limit" (Psalm 147:4–5).

If you understand that God is in control, and you believe that he has a divine plan for everything that happens to your family, then you can start to unpeel your fingers from the tight grasp that you've had on your family's story. You can start to imagine a life that is more than simply surviving what seems like a cosmic accident or a spiritual test, and a place where this thing that once filled you with fear can become the thing that draws you and your child into a deeper relationship with your Creator.

Part 3

THRIVING

9

"No Strings Attached"

Greg

PEOPLE WHO HEAR OUR story today often ask us how we came to reconcile what we read in Scripture—specifically those "clobber verses"—with our changing attitudes toward the LGBTQ community. The common perception, after all, is that the Bible is not kind to homosexuality.

But when I look back, our path toward a ministry of reconciliation happened not *in spite of* the Bible, but *because of it*. Through the years when we were just trying to survive what life handed us, we read Scripture more deeply, and with more passion, than ever before. And God blessed us for it. The more time we spent searching for answers in the Word and the less time we spent listening to outside human opinions, the more God revealed how he wanted us to live. He unraveled for us that what Jesus commands us to do (and it is a command, not a suggestion) is neither complicated nor confusing. But it is pretty radical.

Year by year, verse by verse, he brought joy back into our lives.

Lynn

WE WERE EMPTY NESTERS now, with Connie recently married and Greg Jr. settled in Chicago, so Greg and I fulfilled a long-held dream to move from our home near Grand Rapids to the small resort town of Harbor Springs, right on the northeastern shore of Lake Michigan. This was where we'd vacationed with our family for years, boating on the lake and exploring the quaint, picture-perfect streets that seemed right out of a Norman Rockwell painting.

But no place short of heaven is perfect. There was a lot that we loved about Harbor Springs, but we missed the good friends in Grand Rapids we'd done life with for years and the challenging, in-depth teaching we'd experienced at our previous churches. Harbor Springs, we discovered, was a small, tightly knit community, and we were outsiders. While we eventually settled into a biblically grounded church home and developed a few genuine friendships, it was still a lonely season.

We could have let that discourage us, but instead we used the loneliness to push us even deeper into the Bible. Together and independently, Greg and I dove into Jesus' red letters almost daily. I found myself praying constantly—not the desperate, heartbroken prayers from the early days of my journey, but a hungry, curious desire to know God's plans and purpose for me.

I was finally ready to stop telling God what my acceptable answers were and to start listening to what he said as truth. And when that happened, God blessed me with a level of life-giving intimacy like nothing I'd experienced before.

Greg

THE MORE LYNN AND I read and prayed, the more God revealed to us. Almost daily, it seems like we discovered some new part of his character or our calling. But it was one passage in the book of Matthew, especially, that hit me like a ton of bricks and changed everything.

There was nothing special about the day I happened to read this passage. I'd heard the verses in sermons and read them in devotionals a hundred times before, but this time it was different.

> Hearing that Jesus had silenced the Sadducees, the Pharisees got together. One of them, an expert in the law, tested him with this question: "Teacher, which is the greatest commandment in the Law?" Jesus replied: "'Love the Lord your God with all your heart and with all your soul and with all your mind.' This is the first and greatest commandment. And the second is like it: 'Love your neighbor as yourself.' *All the Law and the Prophets hang on these two commandments*" (Matthew 22:34–40, emphasis added).

I dug a little deeper and discovered that there were 613 laws in the Jewish tradition, which were all based directly or indirectly on God's instructions in the earliest books of what we call the Old Testament. To be in good standing with God, first-century Jews believed that a person had to keep all 613 laws, from the way they wore their hair to the way they prayed. Men like the Pharisees and Sadducees dedicated their entire lives to studying and enforcing those rules as a way to serve and show honor to their Creator.

Albert Einstein once said, "Beyond complexity lies simplicity." Trying to follow 613 rules was complex, just like trying to parent a child—any child—is complex. But here in Matthew, God makes what once seemed complex very simple, yet far more demanding.

Love God and love others. That was it. Those were the core instructions, the things that bring us close to God's plan. Everything else is periphery.

You can almost hear Jesus saying, "If this were a one-hundred-question exam and you only got these two questions correct, you'd pass the exam. If you got the other ninety-eight questions correct and missed these two, you'd fail."

This truth, on top of what Lynn and I had already discovered about "who is your neighbor," changed everything for me. God did not put me on this planet to judge other people's compliance with 613 laws of right behavior. Nor was it up to me to hold someone else to the straight-and-narrow path that I believed God lay out for me. He put me here to love whoever he put in my path, and then to step back and let him do the rest.

And if all he wants from us is a commitment to love him

and our neighbors, how much more are we supposed to love our own children?

Lynn

GREG AND I TALKED about this idea for weeks, turning it around and evaluating it for truth. We sought advice from pastors and theologians we knew and respected.

For years we'd been trying to walk a narrow line, staying true to both what we thought the church taught and what our family needed. Even as we'd entered our son's world, I'd worried that enforcing biblical standards as I understood them would crush our relationship, or that my love for my child would lead me away from God's plan.

Could I love God and love my son? If I loved one, was I turning my back on the other? If I supported Greg Jr. as he lived his life as a gay man, was I somehow endorsing his sexual orientation and disobeying God?

Now it felt like my spiritual foundation was shifting beneath me, and it was really important that we get this right. Greg and I spent hours in prayer, genuinely asking God to show us if we were being led astray.

In the end, we kept coming to the same conclusion, grounded in Scripture and blessed by the Holy Spirit: God doesn't make us choose *people* or *faith*. In fact, he commands that we choose both. Love God *and* love others. The real question was not *How can I love and accept my son in spite of my faith?* but *Because of my faith, how can I not love him?*

To God, people are always more important than the rules.

Or, as Jesus himself said: "The Sabbath was made to meet the needs of people, and not people to meet the requirements of the Sabbath" (Mark 2:27). It never mattered to him whether the people in front of him were sinners or saints, rulers or outcasts. Time after time, he brushed aside "the rules" and offered himself. He didn't demand anything from others—not repentance, not right behavior, and certainly not compliance with "the rules"—in order to experience his love. He didn't care about his reputation or being misunderstood. Instead, he showered those with the worst reputations with mercy, compassion, and grace. He did life with them right where they were, and he showed them what true love looked like.

Oh, I thought, how it must grieve the heart of Jesus to see the wedges driven into relationships because of a person's sexuality—and even more when that relationship is broken in his name! That, I now knew, was not at all what God wanted.

"Okay God," I finally said one afternoon, "I let go. He's yours. I trust you to lead Greg Jr. on the path you choose for him. I'm going to love, no strings attached."

Greg

LOVING GREG JR. AND the LGBTQ community wholeheartedly ended up taking us to some interesting places, whether we believed we were ready for them or not. But then again, people like Moses and Jonah didn't think they were ready for what God was calling them to do, either.

About the same time we moved to Harbor Springs, we also invested in a second home, this one right in the heart of Chicago.

Greg Jr. was still in college, and so we were paying his living expenses. Renting an apartment for him in Chicago was expensive, though, and his place was so small that when Lynn and I visited, we had to stay in a nearby hotel. After a few years of this, we realized that it would be cheaper to invest in a two-bedroom condo that would appreciate in value. When Greg Jr. graduated, he could begin building equity for himself.

Since Greg Jr. would be the primary resident, we let him take the lead in finding the place for us. I wasn't surprised when he chose Boystown, a north Chicago neighborhood that was the first officially recognized LGBTQ neighborhood in the United States. Boystown had quite a reputation. Every June, more than a million people crowd its streets for Chicago's annual Pride Parade, and even on a normal weekend, the marketing campaigns promise that the party never stops.

A decade earlier, I would have refused to visit, much less invest in, a neighborhood where men casually held hands or kissed on the street. I would have flinched at every rainbow flag hanging from an apartment window. It would have been too far outside my comfort zone.

One of the things that had been really pressing on our hearts was the realization that many of us in the Christian church—acting with the best of intentions—had separated and isolated ourselves. We worked, worshipped, lived near, and socialized only with people who believed what we did, looked like we did, and lived like we did. Our vocabularies were the same. Our assumptions were the same. No wonder it was so uncomfortable for us to think about someone who saw the world through a different lens.

On the other hand, every time I went to Scripture, I found another place where Jesus chose to put himself in places that seemed, on the surface, uncomfortable. He didn't spend all his time in the temple. Instead, he took his ministry to the streets. He hung out with tax collectors, prostitutes, lepers, and Gentiles. He talked with people who were very rich and those who were very poor. He traveled far from his neighborhood in Galilee. And everywhere he went, he didn't go looking for the "good" people or those who lived like he did. Instead, Jesus dove right in wherever people were with meals, kindness, and hugs for the children.

I think it was important for Lynn and I to have so many positive examples and Christian mentors around us when we were new Christians. But now, after decades of living a sheltered existence, God was calling us to look past our comfortable walls and preconceived ideas. If Jesus did life with all kinds of people, so would we.

Lynn told me, "If we're going to be serious about loving the LGBTQ community, this is exactly where God is calling us to be."

God had been doing a number on our hearts for years, and so when the right condo opened up in the heart of Boystown, we said yes. If we were going to understand our son and love him and his friends for who they were, Boystown was where that would happen.

Lynn

AT THE TIME, GREG was working for a Christian organization that had an office near Chicago, so we traveled to the condo periodically. During the week, he would "reverse commute" to the suburbs in the morning and come back to the city at night. There were some raised eyebrows among his evangelical co-workers when they found out he was staying in Boystown, but we were both way past the point where we tried to hide our story. This was where God called us to be, and we didn't care who knew it.

While Greg worked, I explored the Lake Michigan beaches and bike paths. Greg Jr. showed me around the neighborhood, which was bordered with rainbow-themed art deco pylons and full of local bookstores, coffee shops, and boutiques. On the surface, a lot of the businesses I saw wouldn't have looked out of place in Harbor Springs, though some of the selections on the bookstore shelves would have raised eyebrows, and there were more than a few sex shops sprinkled among the family-friendly bakeries and gift stores.

It took a while for me to get used to seeing so many same-sex couples on the street, but I think it also took *them* a while to get used to *us*. There weren't many straight, middle-aged, evangelical Christians in Boystown when we arrived in 2009.

SPENDING MORE TIME IN Chicago also meant spending more time with Greg Jr. and Jon, and Lynn and I watched their relationship grow.

Lynn and I liked Jon from the first time we met him, and we came to love him as part of our family. But that didn't stop us from having concerns about whether Greg Jr. and Jon were in the same place, spiritually. Lynn has already shared that as parents, our top priority is always our children's spiritual lives. That included the desire that if either of our kids was going to put in the work to build a relationship, that they would have the reward of eternity together.

When we met Jon, he told us that he was agnostic. This concerned us, and Greg Jr. heard us out when we expressed our thoughts. But once Lynn and I said our piece, we stepped back. *Remember,* we could almost hear God whisper, *love with no strings attached. Trust me with this.*

GREG JR. AND JON got serious enough to move in together, which led to another round of adjustments for Greg and me. We have very traditional views on sex and living together outside of marriage, and so our son's choice was hard to embrace. At the same time, marriage wasn't an option for Greg Jr. Illinois wouldn't pass a same-sex marriage law until 2014, and even then, the idea of marriage as a moral alternative for a gay couple was complicated.

Your job is just to love them, I reminded myself. Again, we expressed our concern to Greg Jr. once and then stepped back and left the situation to God. Jon was part of the family now, just as much as Connie's husband, Matt, and we would love him for who he was and where he was.

For us, being part of the family meant being part of the family Christmas card, so that fall we included Jon in our professional family portrait, which Greg and I had printed onto a few hundred Christmas cards. The message inside read "Love, love, love, and then love some more . . ." above the Matthew 22 Greatest Commandment passage.

A few days before Christmas, we were with Greg Jr. and Jon in New York City, and Jon noticed the last stack of cards on the desk in our hotel room, waiting to be stamped and mailed.

"See?" said Greg Jr. "I told you they were sending them."

It turned out that Jon thought that we included him in the family photo shoot to make him feel good, but that we surely weren't really going to send that card to all our evangelical and politically conservative friends.

Was there a risk in what we did? Maybe. Many Christian parents we know have experienced painful losses of their community and even their livelihoods when their children "came out" of the closet and publicly acknowledged their LGBTQ child's same-sex partner or their transgender child's transition. Many churches and Christian organizations find it uncomfortable to employ a family outside the traditional norm. To avoid possible controversy, they reassign or outright fire a parent who openly acknowledges and loves their LGBTQ child.

But in our case, our political and conservative friends mostly did nothing. A dozen or so friends reached out to say they loved the card, and they wanted to know more about this person who stole Greg Jr.'s heart. To be honest, most people didn't comment on our card at all in the rush of their holiday schedules. If anyone took offense, they kept it to themselves. And that's fine. Greg and I didn't send the card looking to make a statement; we were simply sharing a picture of the family God blessed us with that year.

Greg

LOVING OUR FAMILY WELL didn't mean I always said or did the right things. A couple of years after that Christmas card, Greg Jr. and Jon came to visit us, and we all took a walk to the dog park. On the way, we ran into a neighbor friend who lived on our street.

I started to introduce them. "This is Jon. He's Greg Jr.'s . . ." I trailed off for a second. *What was the appropriate word in this situation?* I wasn't sure how our neighbor would react, or even how my son wanted his relationship explained. "Partner," I finished, somewhat lamely. The moment felt awkward for all of us.

Good intentions, I learned, needed to be attached to intentional actions. I needed to be proactive and ask my son for guidance. How did he refer to Jon? What would he like me to say when I introduced them?

The next time, I was smoother with my introductions, and the time after that, I didn't think twice when I said, "This is Greg Jr.'s boyfriend." (That, I'd learned, was the word they preferred; to them, *partner* sounded like it was a business arrangement.)

It turns out that the cliché is wrong, and even old dogs can learn new tricks.

For years, Satan had been interfering with my family and my faith. He'd crowded in on my relationships and made me think terrible things about people I loved. But now I was fighting back with love, following Jesus' example. And I have to say, it felt good.

Lynn

THE YEARS PASSED, AND we kept going to Boystown. Visiting Greg Jr. meant that we had more chances to hang out and interact with his friends, often joining them for fun, noisy dinners and binge-watching TV shows.

As we got to know Greg Jr.'s friends, both straight and gay, we started to learn their stories. Some of them were inspiring, like a loyal, soft-spoken friend of Greg's named Nick, who went on to be a successful lawyer. Or Nina, a beautiful young lady who lost her dad sometime after we met her. Nina was one of the first to ask if Greg and I would be her "adopted parents," and we agreed wholeheartedly. She immediately began referring to us affectionately as McMom and McDad.

The more we listened to these young people, the more we began to understand how much hurt there was in the LGBTQ community. We saw how many times men and women we'd come to love had been rejected, attacked, and denied, and even worse, how often those wounds came at the hands of Christian family members and churches.

When they found out that Greg and I were followers of Christ, some of our new friends told us about the church groups that stood along the parade route at the Pride Festival with signs that said, "God hates you and you're going to hell" and worse. What could we say to that, other than to assure them that Jesus would never act like that? Jesus didn't hate anyone.

Mother Teresa once said, "Being unwanted, unloved, un-cared for, forgotten by everybody, I think that is a much greater hunger, a much greater poverty than the person who has nothing to eat." I thought about her words often as I struggled to know how to respond. Over and over I found myself wanting to apologize for the people who claimed to act in the name of the Jesus I served yet who left so many of these people Jesus loved wounded in their wake. I felt guilty by association.*

---

*Not all of the stories coming out at the time were bad. We lived in Boystown at about the same time that young Christians such as Andrew Marin, also a Boystown resident and founder of the Marin Foundation, started attending pride parades with signs that apologized for how Christians have treated gay people over the years. His "I'm Sorry" campaign has reached millions, both inside the LGBTQ community and around the world, with a message of hope and Christ's love.

Greg

WE GOT TO KNOW one young man, Jared, especially well. He told Lyhn and me that he was eighteen when his mom learned he was gay. She didn't handle it well. In fact, she told him that she wished he'd never been born, and they hadn't spoken in almost ten years. He cried as he told us his story, and our hearts broke. When he asked if we would consider being his "adopted parents," once again we couldn't agree fast enough. This "McMom" and "McDad" thing was getting traction.

This is why you're here, I heard God whisper as Lynn and I hugged our new "son." To love our neighbors in every way possible, to live out the promise of Psalm 68:6 that "God sets the lonely in families," and to be parents to those whose parents abandoned them.

The further along Lynn and I get in our journey, the more we see the importance of family, and how often the lack of one has left our LGBTQ friends lost and in pain. It's through healthy families that we learn what it means to belong. Families assure us that we are neither alone nor abandoned. Someone is on our side who cares. Someone loves us. When those things are ripped away, as happens far too often with LGBTQ youth, the wounds are deep. Wherever we could, we stepped in to fill the gap. Today, dozens of young adults all across the country call us McMom and McDad, titles we cherish.

Jared called us several months later and asked us to pray for him. He was feeling a lot of fear as he was being prepped for surgery on his back, and he longed for a feeling of connectedness. Being able to pray with him and bring his fear to God was a privilege.

This wasn't a chore. This was no longer a mission field; this was becoming our lives' passion.

Lynn

GOD'S WORK ON OUR hearts was dramatic. God continued to show me how much I had in common with my gay, lesbian, bisexual, and transgender friends. It was impossible to equate these sweet, smart, sensitive people with that anonymous "gay agenda" that used to fill me with fear. These were men and women created in the image of God, just like me.

Greg and I no longer fought each other over what had "broken" our son. Now we worked together to get to know him, the *real* him, in a new way. Our marriage deepened as we read the Bible and sought God together.

"You know," I told a family member one day, "I'm so thankful that God gave me a gay son." She responded with a look of confusion and disbelief. She'd tolerated my conversations about my family, but it was clear that she struggled with how to react.

"I'm serious," I told her. No, this wasn't the life I would have chosen for him. And actually, Greg Jr. has often said that this isn't the life he would have chosen for himself. Being gay has often been a painful, lonely experience for him, but I'm increasingly convinced that God put us all here for a reason. God used Greg Jr. to work miracles in my heart.

I told her that I would never have come to this place if the closest LGBTQ person to me was a friend's son, or a cousin, or someone else more removed. I had to love someone so deeply that I was willing to change the way I saw the world through my comfortable North American Christian lens.

God knew that, of course, long before I did.

Key Learnings: Make It Personal

+ Look for places in your relationship with your child where you are still "holding the strings" or trying to control their behavior. Ask yourself if there is anything in your parenting that you're still holding back from God's control, perhaps thinking that it's up to you to protect or change your child. In prayer, ask God to help you let go of those things, and step into a new level of trust.

+ If you are wondering how to love your child well, especially if the tension has been building in your family for a long time, here are some practical, effective ways that we've seen families connect with an LGBTQ son or daughter:

     + Ask your child what he wished you knew about them.

     + Ask your adult child what it was like growing up in your home. (The answer may be painful, but it can be a platform to stimulate honest conversation and healing.)

+ Even if you are estranged, send birthday cards and notes of encouragement.

+ Find things to talk about other than your child's orientation or gender identity. What are the things that you all enjoy? Engage them about sports, cooking, or the latest TV shows you're binge-watching.

+ Talk to them about what's going on in their life. Be careful not to assume that all your child's struggles are related to their sexual orientation or gender identity. Gay and straight people alike go through similar struggles, and your child's sexual identity is only one part of their being.

+ Find your child's love language. Gary Chapman's book *The 5 Love Languages* (or *A Teen's Guide to the 5 Love Languages*) is a good resource to help you identify how your child receives love. Whether it's gifts, words of affirmation, acts of service, quality time, or physical touch, focus your energy on what your child will understand as a sign of love.

+ Don't stop praying. Wherever your child is spiritually, continue to pray that they move one step closer to

Jesus. Ask God to bring Christian men and women into your child's life to encourage their walk and for your family relationships to grow in unity. Only God knows how and whether your child should change, or how their choices will work for his greater plan.

+ Don't limit your actions because of worry that embracing your LGBTQ child and their friends will somehow make it look to others like you are condoning their behavior or changing your core beliefs. By this point, your child and the people who are close to you should already know how both biblical principles and family values guide your life. And if a person or organization shuns you because of your love and support for your family, pray for the grace to forgive them and make more time for the people who love you unconditionally.

10

"The Game Changer"

Lynn

"I'M SO GLAD THAT God gave me a gay son." I can't overstate what a radical change my life had taken for me to be able to say this. The part of my family that I once wanted to hide—now I wanted to tell everyone I met about what God was teaching me through it.

But even that became a lesson.

"Mom," Greg Jr. told me more than once, "I'm tired of you referring to me as your 'gay son.' I'm the only son you've got, and I'm more than one thing. I'm your son, but I'm also a brother. I'm a neighbor. I'm a friend, I'm a citizen, I'm an employee. You don't go around talking about your 'straight daughter' like that."

He had a good point. Even as I came to appreciate what made my son uniquely himself, I was still filtering everything about Greg Jr. through this one lens.

As we've met more parents of LGBTQ children over the

years, I've learned that my initial fixation is fairly common. When there is one unexpected facet of our child's identity, it can easily overshadow all the other things that make them unique. We start to filter everything through the lens of this one part of their identity, and it becomes easy to forget to see their other strengths and wonderful God-given qualities.

My son was much more than "my gay son," but it took another major life upheaval for me to fully appreciate that.

Greg

IN 2012, CONNIE AND her husband, Matt, were living in Atlanta, where they'd moved for work reasons. Their four-year-old son, our first grandchild, had captured a huge slice of our hearts. When Connie mentioned that she and Matt were thinking about expanding their family and they asked if we would ever consider moving to be closer to them, Lynn and I took the invitation seriously and committed ourselves to a lot of prayer.

Moving to Atlanta would be a huge change for us. We'd both lived our entire lives in Michigan, and most of our friends and family lived there. Plus, moving to Atlanta would put us farther away from Greg Jr. in Chicago.

But in the end, who could say no to the chance to live near a grandchild and his parents? We would be close to a major airport, we reasoned, which kept Chicago just a nonstop flight and a few hours away.

Lynn and I traded small-town life in northern Michigan

for the busy Atlanta suburb of Duluth, Georgia, once named a "top ten city for American values."

Then the floor dropped out from under us.

Just a few weeks after we arrived in Georgia, with all of our boxes and furniture, we went back to Grand Rapids to visit friends and tie up a few loose ends. Because we hadn't selected new doctors in Atlanta yet, Lynn took advantage of the chance to go to her familiar Michigan physician for her annual physical. Her routine mammogram showed a suspicious spot, which led to more testing and a biopsy.

Those days of waiting were a scary time for us, coming just a few years after my mom had died from breast cancer that metastasized to the bone. We were staying with friends, and I was in the car, on the way to pick up ingredients to make dinner for us all, when the doctor's office called. Lynn had been feeling anxious about what the test would show, so she'd given them my number to call with the results.

I pulled to the side of the road and listened as a kind nurse explained what the test had shown. The day turned suddenly surreal, straight out of *The Twilight Zone,* as I turned around and went back to the house, my dinner plans forgotten.

I woke Lynn up from a nap. "I'm so sorry," I said, wanting to hold her and protect her from what was coming. "The doctor found cancer in your breast."

ONCE AGAIN, MY LIFE changed in an instant. Right away, we had to make a big decision. Atlanta is an incredible city with some of the finest health care anywhere in the country, but we didn't know a soul in the medical community there. In contrast, we were friends with many fabulous doctors in West Michigan who could help us assemble a top-flight team. On the other hand, staying in Michigan meant facing months of surgeries, chemotherapy, radiation, and reconstruction without a home base. This was one of those moments when we needed God to step in, and he did, in a very big way.

Without us ever having to ask, our friends Doug and Gina offered to let us use a condo they owned so we would have a place to live during my treatments. During the time when their home was already committed, our dear friends Jan and Jerry—that same couple who were the first people we told when we found out Greg Jr. was gay—offered their home. This was the Body of Christ in action, showering our family with love and practical support at the time we needed it most.

In the weeks that followed, Greg and I had a crash course in cancer. I chose to have a bilateral (double) mastectomy, and during that surgery they found cancer cells in a lymph node, so they removed thirteen additional lymph nodes.

Then things got really hard. My biopsy results put me right on the edge of what's called triple negative cancer, which is very aggressive. That was terrifying, but my oncologist assured us that she thought we'd caught it in time, and if she threw "the big guns" at it, we could kill it all.

WHEN THEY SAID "WE'LL give it everything we have," what they really meant was "this treatment is going to take Lynn to the point of feeling like she's on the brink of death, but it will be worth it." The oncologist's "big guns" were a potent sixteen-week chemo regimen, followed by radiation.

Those months were brutal. The effects of chemo built over time. After the first treatment, Lynn said, "That's not so bad." And then the second was a little harder, and the one after that was worse. The sixteenth week of chemo was simply awful. It took absolutely everything out of her.

Lynn and I put every other part of our lives—all the appointments, decisions, and to-do lists that used to seem so important—on hold and dedicated ourselves, 100 percent, to beating this thing physically, mentally, and spiritually. I was with Lynn for every appointment and treatment, doing whatever I could while she bore the physical and emotional pain.

For me, the hardest thing was the inability to control the outcome. God had been working on my life for years, teaching me to let go and trust him with my kids, but this was *my wife.* Lynn was my life partner of thirty-six years, I was totally smitten with her, and it broke my heart to see her suffer. I wanted to fix things. I was good at fixing things. For years, my work partners called me "the firefighter," because I was the guy who could parachute into a raging fire to restore a situation when a client, customer, or branch office had big issues. But I didn't have the tools to fight a fire like this.

Lynn

IT WAS AMAZING HOW my whole family just surrounded me that year. Greg was with me every day, through everything, and so were the kids.

In between rounds of chemo in Michigan, Greg and I went to Chicago and stayed in the Boystown condo with Greg Jr. and Jon. Even at my weakest points, I wanted to be close to my family.

But being with my kids brought new kinds of challenges. As a mom, I've always believed that it's my job to nurture my children and take care of them. When cancer came, I couldn't be that caretaker. Most of the time, it was hard enough just to stay awake. For a long time, I would wake up, brush my teeth, eat breakfast, and go back to sleep.

In the time of my weakness, my son became my caretaker. When I would nap on the couch, Greg Jr. would put a blanket on me. He would fold my laundry. I remember lying there, watching my son fold my underwear, and thinking *That's supposed to be my job as the mom. He shouldn't have to do that.* But he graciously did it anyway.

For the first time in more than a decade, when I looked at him I didn't think about Greg Jr. as "my gay son." His sexuality didn't make a bit of difference to me when I was at my weakest point. He was simply my son, one of the people I loved most in the world, and he was taking care of me. I saw Jesus so much in him, and in all of my family. I just wanted to stay alive so that I could love them all more and build deeper relationships with them.

CANCER WAS A GAME changer on every level for our entire family. It rocked our world. It made us step back and ask tough questions about God, but it also opened us up to see his deep love for us in new ways, and it drew us together.

For Lynn and me, one of the greatest gifts was watching both of our kids reach out to care for their mom.

Greg Jr. and Connie always had a good relationship, but as adults living hundreds of miles apart, they didn't talk all that often. Not long after Lynn received the diagnosis, though, Greg Jr. called Connie. "Hey, we have to distract Mom. She needs things to think about other than cancer."

Together, they developed a plan. Connie was expecting her second child by then, and she enlisted Lynn in coming up with names for the baby, who was due to arrive in five months. She would call and email new ideas all the time, asking for Lynn's input and keeping her focused on the future. Greg Jr., meanwhile, kept Lynn busy with decorating questions for our new house in Atlanta. Every other day, it seemed to me, he'd have a new fabric swatch or pictures of furniture for her to consider. He also took the lead in researching what would happen when Lynn lost her hair as a result of the chemo. He realized long before we did that Lynn would need hats to stay warm, even inside. I don't know how many different hats and scarves they ended up picking out together, but I know that dreaming about the future with her son encouraged her.

Lynn

THAT'S THE THING ABOUT families. We spend a lot of time worrying and disagreeing about the small things until something big comes and washes it all away. It doesn't have to be cancer. Families are rocked by illness, accidents, addictions, job loss, financial crises, and more.

One day, we're all going about our day-to-day business, and our biggest concern is what people at church will think of us if our kid wears *that shirt* on Sunday or how we'll finish the report that our boss asked for. The next, everything has been turned upside down. Priorities change.

If you're a parent standing beside an unconscious child's hospital bed, the way our friend Linda Robertson was, it stops mattering whether they're straight or gay, male or female. All that matters is that they live.*

If you get a phone call from a police officer and it starts, "I'm sorry, but there's been an accident," you forget about the argument you had with your spouse that morning about coming home on time, and you frantically wonder if you said, "I love you" when they walked out the door.

And if you find out some of your own cells are trying to kill you, then you don't worry anymore about whether your house looks nice enough or whether your kid behaves like other people's kids.

---

*You'll find a link to Linda's incredible story and her blog *Just Because He Breathes* at www.justbecausehebreathes.com. But I warn you—keep the tissues handy. Her testimony is a heartbreaker.

Greg

OUR FAMILY SHARED A lot during that year, but we also each went through our own private journey of tears and fears. At one point while we were in Boystown and Lynn was napping, Greg Jr. suggested that he and I go out for a drink.

He took me to a local pub just kitty-corner from our condo called the Closet. As I walked in, I realized that it was a gay bar. There was a time when I would have gotten stuck on that idea. What would my friends and coworkers think if they saw me in here? But now, I had bigger things to worry about.

As we talked, Greg Jr. told me, "I've prayed more in the last month than I have in the last five years combined." I was thrilled Greg allowed me that small glimpse into his spiritual life, something he had been very closed about after being wounded by so many people in the church.

God does bring gifts along with the suffering.

Lynn

CANCER DIDN'T JUST MAKE us aware of the bigger issues. It also gave us new perspectives on the things that we'd been engaged with for a long time.

A few months into my chemo treatments I was having one of those afternoons when I just felt sorry for myself. I had lost all my hair by that point, including my eyebrows and eyelashes, and I thought I sort of looked like an alien.

Greg Jr. had helped me pick out a beautiful natural hair

wig that matched my real hairstyle, color, and texture. But whenever I went out, I could tell that people stared at me. They treated me differently. No one was ever mean—in fact, I thought most people were kinder and more sympathetic than usual—but I also felt a distance between me and the rest of the world, and a lot of pity. I was not like them.

I always felt on edge, like I was on display.

As I stood in front of the mirror feeling sorry for myself about not fitting in anymore, God reminded me that others were also alienated, but they weren't treated with kindness. I thought of our openly gay, lesbian, and transgender friends, and how when they went out, people stopped and stared, or distanced themselves. Some people even looked at them with disgust, like they were aliens.

My experience was temporary. I knew my hair would eventually grow back, and this "alien" stage would eventually end. I'd go back to fitting in. But many of the people I loved would always look a little different when they went out. Walking down the street, and facing the reactions of others, would always take courage.

Greg

IF WE WEREN'T THERE already, cancer pushed us over the edge of our commitment to radically love whoever God put in our path.

Life was shorter than I realized, and my propensity for judging others dried up completely. When Lynn was sick, literally hundreds of prayer warriors surrounded us. They were straight, gay, and transgender. They were men and women, baby boomers and millennials, wealthy and not.

Every one of them was God's unique creation, someone created in God's own image, someone who deserved love and respect, someone Jesus loved enough to die for. Every one of them loved my family enough to hold us up in prayer while we battled. And whether God gave me two more years on this earth or fifty, I was going to spend it digging deep with people, investing myself in human connections more than anything else.

Lynn

WE SPENT CHRISTMAS AT home in Georgia, and then there was radiation, and complications from radiation, followed by more surgeries and many more months of healing.

I felt like a ticking time bomb. If my particular type of cancer was going to recur and metastasize, my oncologist said, it would normally happen within five years. And so I rested, exercised, ate right, and waited.

And I prayed. Oh, how I prayed. *God, don't let this experience happen to me for no reason. Show me your purpose here.*

My life was a gift, something I didn't take for granted anymore. So much of the pride I wrestled with and the secrecy I once held about having a gay son had been stripped away. The things that once kept me from loving my son were nothing but a distant memory. I had been given a new lease on life, and I became committed to living in a way that made a difference.

Key Learnings: Make It Personal

+ Know that you are not invincible. At some point, you will face a "game changer" moment in your family. A medical diagnosis, an accident, or something else truly life-threatening will affect your priorities, your perception of time, and your love for your family. Hold the present gently, because it may change tomorrow. Let go of your grudges. Ask God to help you unclench your fingers from the things that don't have eternal value.

+ When a crisis does upend your world, don't try to handle everything alone. This is why God put us in communities and families, to support and encourage each other during the hard times. Don't hesitate to ask for both prayer and practical support when you need it.

+ If your family is going through a crisis, talk to your children about how they are processing the experience. Be honest about the things you worry about and struggle with and ask them to share their thoughts with you.

11

"There's Someone Who Needs to Talk to You"

Greg

THE FIRST CALL CAME when Greg Jr. was still in college, years before Lynn's cancer was even on our radar.

"I have a good friend, and she just found out that her daughter is gay. She and her husband are devastated and have no idea what to do. Would you be willing to talk to her?"

It happened not long after my mom passed away. She was an amazing lady and a real fighter. No matter how ill she got from the cancer that was eating her alive, my mom refused chemotherapy, and eventually her cancer metastasized to her bones. At first, I asked her, over and over, to reconsider taking chemotherapy. I wanted her to keep fighting her disease with all the ammunition available to her. But she would shake her finger at me and say, "Listen, buster"—she loved to call me "buster" when she was frustrated with me—"until you've walked in the shoes of the Fisherman, you don't know. You don't know what I'm going through, and so you can't know what I should do." She was right, of course.

Well, when it came to the confused emotions of being a Christian parent with an LGBTQ child, Lynn and I *did* know what others were going through, and so of course we said yes and met with the family that needed support. And when another family called a few months later, we said yes to them as well. And then to the couple after that.

As I've said before, one of the hardest parts of learning to parent a gay child is the sense that we are traveling through a minefield alone. Lynn and I had desperately wanted someone to talk to, someone who could relate to our story, during those early years. There was no way we were going to turn down the chance to be that listening ear for someone else.

We were still making plenty of mistakes as parents of an LGBTQ child, but we'd also learned a lot along the way, and we had something more important than answers. We had experience and compassion.

Lynn

FOR YEARS, I'D ASSUMED that God was calling me to a ministry of sharing the gospel with the gay community. Instead, God was gently leading us to their parents, people like us who believed in Christ already, but who were wrestling with how to live out their faith and take care of their families.

Greg and I didn't have a plan or a script for when the phone rang (or, increasingly, as the emails arrived). We instinctively knew that our presence, not our answers, was the greatest gift we could offer. So, we offered meals, quiet places, hugs, tears, and lots of prayer. We learned to be quick to listen and slow to speak. When we did speak, we asked lots of questions, and we shared our unvarnished story openly, allowing moms and dads to hear what God had done in our lives, as well as the questions we were still asking.

God orchestrated everything so naturally that I hardly even noticed what was happening. But one afternoon, in the middle of a Fourth of July party at our Harbor Springs home, I was talking casually about how God was opening doors for us to help others. "Someone even suggested that I write a book about our story," I said.

Our friend Steve gave me a long look. "Are you ready to be the face of this?"

I knew right away what he meant.

It was one thing to meet a few couples face-to-face and share our story in safe places. But was I really willing to "go public"?

Our commitment to love our son and his friends had already created a barrier in some of our relationships. What would happen if Greg and I became more vocal about our experience? We might get battered from both sides.

The Christian church is full of people who genuinely believe that the Bible calls them to separate from and judge those in the LGBTQ community, who they view as sinful and outside God's direction.

Meanwhile, there are lots of people in the lesbian, gay, bisexual, and transgender community who have been so wounded by Christians that they push away anyone who comes to them in the name of Jesus. Many of them want nothing to do with God.

Was God asking me to jump into the middle of the culture war?

When I told Greg about the conversation, his immediate reaction was "bring it on." His heart was fully engaged with healing the hurt between the two communities we loved, regardless of the cost. I was hesitant, though. It wasn't until cancer stripped everything away that I was ready to see our calling as something bigger than what could happen at my kitchen table.

Greg

LYNN AND I HAD no idea when we relocated to Atlanta how God would use the move to expand our ministry and change our lives.

One of our first priorities when we arrived was to plug into a church where we could serve. We were initially drawn to North Point Community Church because of Pastor Andy Stanley's teaching. After all, it was his father Charles who had been so influential in bringing Lynn and me to Christ thirty years before. And we knew from Connie and Matt that North Point was a fully alive, rapidly growing, Bible-based community—just what we were looking for. So right away, Lynn and I started to worship at North Point Community Church.

We knew that we'd made the right choice when, not long after we arrived, Andy Stanley made national headlines for a talk he gave at a convention of pastors. He said, "We just need to decide from now on in our churches when a middle-school kid comes out to his small-group leader, or a high school young lady comes out to her parents . . . We just need to decide, regardless of what you think about this topic—no more students are going to feel like they have to leave the local church because they're same-sex attracted or because they're gay. That ends with us."*

He caught some flak for that statement from Christians who argued that the compassion he described was actually accommodating a sinful culture. Andy's words, though, were a lifeline for families like ours, who knew firsthand the importance of churches becoming the "safest place on the planet for students to talk about anything, including same-sex attraction." Those kids existed, whether people in the pews liked it or not, and the church wasn't helping them (or their families) grow closer to Jesus by denying their existence or telling them they weren't welcome.

Any Christian family with an LGBTQ member knows the challenge of finding a biblically grounded church that is balanced in both truth and grace, and dedicated to making a difference, not a point. We long for places that do not water down the scriptures, but don't use them as weapons either. Where staff and volunteers are both approachable and engaged.

The local body of believers should be the ultimate "safe place" where every person—young and old, male and female,

---

*"Pastor Andy Stanley Says Churches Should Be a Safe Place for Gay Youth," *Christian Today*, April 20, 2015, https://www.christiantoday.com/article/pastor-andy-stanley-says-churches-should-be-a-safe-place-for-gay-youth/52441.htm.

gay and straight—can wrestle with their faith and the big questions of their lives. It should be a place that welcomes the kind of outsiders Jesus loved, and engages them with both love and the core principles of theology.

At North Point, we found all of that. For the first time in many years, it felt like our whole family, including Greg Jr. and Jon, were welcome to worship together.

Lynn

THERE ARE LOTS OF media reports about how millennials, born in the 1980s and '90s, are more open than any generation before them to accepting homosexuality as part of their culture. They're more likely to identify as LGBTQ, and they're coming out at younger ages, even in the evangelical church community.[*]

What that means, Greg and I discovered, is that there are a lot of non-millennial Christian parents trying to adjust to radical changes in their cultural and family landscapes. Every week, we talked to moms and dads all across the country, each of them going through their own journeys with LGBTQ family members. Many of them were still in those shell-shocked, fear-filled early days of their journey. Often, we were the first people they'd ever shared their thoughts and fears with.

---

[*]Robert P. Jones and Daniel Cox, "How Race and Religion Shape Millennial Attitudes on Sexuality and Reproductive Health," March 27, 2015, https://www.prri.org/wp-content/uploads/2015/03/PRRI-Millennials-Web-FINAL.pdf.

Looking back, I'm amazed to see how God gently, over time, prepared us for our life calling. He orchestrated each of the steps that brought me from that attitude of "what happens in this house stays in this house" to the place where what I valued most was transparency and honesty. As one family became ten, and ten became dozens, I got used to sharing our story, and eventually there was nothing about us that was secret anymore.

We knew God was using our experiences to help others, and it felt good that it wasn't wasted. But we still didn't have a plan, or any idea how big God's vision for this really was.

Greg

FOR MANY YEARS, I'D been on the board of a ministry called Orphan Helpers, a ministry for kids in El Salvador and Honduras. One weekend, one of the Orphan Helpers executives, a great guy named Ron, came with his wife, Barb, to visit us in Atlanta.

He mentioned that he'd set up a breakfast meeting with Bill Willits, an executive director and one of the original founders of North Point Ministries. Ron invited me to come to the breakfast to represent the Orphan Helpers board, which I was happy to do.

During the meal, one thing led to another, and I mentioned that my wife and I were doing informal ministry with families of LGBTQ children, based on our own experience. Both of the North Point men were captivated by my story of reaching out to and loving the families around us. When I left that day, Bill asked if he could follow up with us.

We discovered that long before Bill ever heard our story, the church had started a series of conversations about how to minister to families in the congregation whose children had recently come out. Bill quickly became a mentor, good friend, and kindred spirit in ministry, and it was clear our meeting had been perfectly timed, a true "God moment."

That first conversation in the church office turned into a series of conversations that continued in the weeks and months that followed, and Lynn and I were impressed by the depth and compassion that the church was bringing to the issue. Still, we were surprised when Bill approached us about sharing our story as part of a video segment North Point was producing for an upcoming conference.

Were we ready to be the face of this? You bet we were. Lynn and I spent a day working with a film crew, talking about the ways God had helped us grow and healed our family. A few weeks later, the edited version of those conversations, complete with our laughter and tears, was shown to more than two thousand pastors and leaders from around the world who were attending the biennial North Point Drive Conference.

As he introduced the clip, Andy Stanley told the assembled group, "This is the reality for those of us who are in ministry . . . We're dealing with real people and real relationships, and real people that we love, so we have to figure this out. It's not political for me; it is not political for you, is it? It's relational, because we're in ministry."

ONE OF THE THINGS we love about our church family is the way that the leadership constantly encourages us to "move toward the mess." North Point's commitment is always about meeting people where they're at while helping them grow in their relationship with Jesus.

One of the ways they do this is through a care ministry called Parent Connect, which seeks to provide a safe, small-group environment where parents of LGBTQ children can experience community and personal growth. Greg and I immediately fell in love with the Parent Connect mission to encourage parents to love their LGBTQ sons and daughters well, while not sacrificing their faith.

Not long after we taped the video message for the Drive conference, Greg and I shared our story at a local Parent Connect meeting, and then we joined the group the following month. Before long, we were asked to facilitate a new Parent Connect group in our home. This kind of personal, relational ministry was right up our alley, and with the church's support, the group grew rapidly. At each monthly meeting, we talk through a few structured, scripturally based questions, and allow plenty of time for parents to talk about the issues they were facing. We've had as many as twenty-five parents come in one evening, and we're just one of the many Parent Connect groups that meet across the Atlanta metro area.

The families we meet, both locally and long distance, have held secrets or walked alone, sometimes for many years, and this is the first time they felt safe to talk to other adults with LGBTQ children. One sweet lady we'll call Susie had not told anyone in seventeen years that her daughter was gay. She remembered the heartbreaking time in the 1980s when her church hired guards on horseback to "protect their property" when the annual gay pride parade passed by. Susie was scared that if anyone from her church or her friends found out her daughter was a lesbian, she herself would no longer be welcome. Finding us was a massive relief for her, because she finally had someone to share her journey with.

Greg

OUR GROWING "KITCHEN TABLE ministry" was a real lifeline for us during those early months in Atlanta.

At the time, I was working in a job that wasn't a good fit for me. Lynn suggested we pray about whether I should leave, and so we did. My prayer was basically, "God, please throw open the door, or slam it shut and give me a bloody nose. But please, don't make me guess."

Two months later, Andy Stanley started a new sermon series at North Point called "Re:Solution" to help people start the new year in a positive way. One of the questions he asked in his kickoff message stuck with me. "What breaks your heart?" he asked. His challenge was that if we really wanted to become better people, we should do something to make the world a better place instead of committing to typical New Year's resolutions.

A few days after the sermon our small group met, and we talked about what breaks our hearts.

Lynn and I hadn't talked about the sermon, but I remember as we sat there that evening we looked at each other, and the answer was obvious. We'd both spent years giving our labor, influence, finances, and expertise to plenty of issues that we deeply cared about, but there was only one thing God had put front and center in our lives that truly broke our hearts.

"The LGBTQ community," I said without hesitation when it was my turn to share. Lynn chimed in, "Exactly." That was the place where God was calling us to make a difference.

Lynn

GREG AND I WERE talking to dozens of Christian parents around the country by then who were all struggling, often alone, with their fears and concerns about an LGBTQ child. They often didn't have the kind of church support we were blessed with, or any church support at all, and the loneliness left their faith dying on the vine.

It was about this time that I read Scot McKnight's *The Jesus Creed*, and one statement in particular jumped out at me: "Nothing is more important for the development of love than being loved—we may be taught the importance to love, but *to experience it is to know it.*"*

---

*Scot McKnight, *The Jesus Creed: Loving God, Loving Others* (Brewster, MA: Paraclete Press, 2014), 107.

There were thousands of families across the country, I knew, who were struggling to know how to love their children and their church community. My heart filled with the sense that Greg and I were in a unique place to help them by offering them the experience of being loved themselves.

Should we change the way we looked at what we were doing? What if we committed more of ourselves to this thing that broke our hearts and made it a full-time focus? Greg and I were trained in discipleship and had almost fifteen years of experience with one-on-one relational ministry by that point. Now it seemed like God was calling us to use our gifts to connect even more families with each other and with the church.

Our prayers shifted from "God, if you want Greg to leave his job, make it clear" to "God, do you want us to pursue this ministry full-time?"

Less than a month later, Greg's boss sat down with him and said, "I'm sorry, but we're consolidating our staff and are eliminating your position." He had a real heart of compassion, and it was clear he regretted having to have the conversation. But all Greg felt was a sense of relief. This was the answer to our prayer. God had given us the sign we'd asked for. Now we just needed to understand what our next steps should look like.

Greg

OVER THE NEXT FEW months, we took a hard look at our lifestyle and made changes so that we could afford to invest in our ministry and live without an income. We downsized our house, sold a car, and got our spending in line. We met with the incredible staff at North Point many times, and they generously offered solid advice, great support, and serious wisdom. In August 2015, we filed the paperwork to make Embracing the Journey Inc. a legally official 501(c)(3) nonprofit organization.

The Lord had been preparing us "for such a time as this" our whole lives, and we were off to the races.

The first step was to expand our network. Embracing the Journey has always been a ministry based on peer-to-peer, one-on-one relationships, and that didn't change. Without relationships, we believe, this is not ministry. But now Lynn and I had a lot more time to give to the people God put in our lives.

Through another connection, we were introduced to the Gay Christian Network, now called Q Christian Fellowship, which provides support to LGBTQ Christians and advocates for stronger relationships between the church and the LGBTQ community. Embracing the Journey didn't even have a website the first time GCN invited us to speak and lead a workshop designed to help parents embrace their journey at their conference.

God was moving fast, and it was fun to see where he was taking us.

Lynn

SPEAKING TO A LARGE group was a nerve-racking experience for me, but I knew it would be worth it to see how God would use our story.

After one of our sessions, a woman came up to us with a man she introduced as Chip. "You're all doing ministry in Atlanta, so I think you need to meet each other," she explained.

We learned that Chip and his husband, Mike, hosted a nondenominational Bible study for the LGBTQ community in their home, and when he invited us to visit the group, we eagerly accepted.

Up to that point, Greg and I hadn't had many opportunities to sit down and connect personally with devout Christ followers who also happened to be LGBTQ. Most of the Christians we met through our ministry were straight parents and church leaders. The LGBTQ friends we'd met through Greg Jr. were all in different places in their spiritual journeys, but few of them were actively pursuing a deeper relationship with Jesus.

There were two dozen folks gathered in a living room, and the first thing I noticed was how excited they all were to dig into the Bible. Here was a group of people who had been told over and over that they were abominations, and that God doesn't love them. Famous Christians publicly said that being gay was enough to send them to hell. And yet they were not dissuaded or discouraged. In many ways, just the opposite happened. They pursued God with passion. The depth of their knowledge humbled me, as did their desire for building a supportive, Christ-centered community.

The second thing I noticed was that Chip and Mike were okay not having all the answers, even about homosexuality. There were people in the group who believed the Bible called them to celibacy, and those who believed that God blessed committed, lifelong same-sex relationships. A few were skeptical about the Bible, exploring Christianity for the first time in a safe space. Many shared that they'd been Christians for decades. Those differences didn't divide them, though. Instead, they focused on what they had in common: their love for God, love for their neighbors, and the desire to be in a relationship with Christ.

This was all eye-opening for me, but the thing that surprised me most during our first time together was myself. By this point, Greg and I had shared the story of how we "outed" Greg Jr., and all the mistakes we'd made, hundreds of times and to groups much larger than this. But as I started to repeat the familiar series of events, I began sobbing.

Talking to a group of people who were LGBTQ was so different from talking to parents or church leaders. As I locked eyes with the men and women I'd once judged so harshly, I was filled with embarrassment. All I could do was apologize, first for crying, and then for what they were about to hear. And then I shared the only way I knew how, honestly and deeply. I didn't hold anything back. I confessed to this group of kind people, some of whom also had tears in their eyes, what I'd once thought about them. How I'd thrown clobber verses and trite clichés at them. How I had begged God not to let my child be like them.

When I was done, they showed me grace and mercy in ways they seldom ever experienced themselves. They hugged me and forgave me. They asked thought-provoking questions about how and why my beliefs changed.

Their response was life-giving to me, and it forever

changed the way I approached others. That night I learned the value of listening to another person's story with an open heart, and I tried to model that back to them. I did a lot of listening that night, and I did a lot of learning. I may have had thirty years of experience as a Christian by that point, but this community of LGBTQ Christians had a lot to teach me.

Greg

IT WAS A CRAZY powerful evening, and over the months that followed God opened the door for many wonderful relationships to form between us and the men and women in Chip's Bible study. They offered us a deep level of trust that flowed, I believe, from our own willingness to be honest with them and not to pretend that we had it all together.

We were long past the place of acting like flawless and shiny Christian parents, and the result was like a magnet to steel: it drew people to offer a deeper level of candid honesty as well.

As we made ourselves more available, God brought more families into our lives. Some of them, like a couple we'll call Kevin and Beth, reached out after their relationship with their son had reached a total free fall. Kevin and Beth had a deep, lifelong faith, and Beth, especially, knew her Bible really well. She and Lynn bonded as fellow "Bible-preaching mamas."

When their son Thomas came out as gay, the couple took it hard. Beth, especially, felt like it was her duty to convict her son of his sin and debate his interpretation of Scripture. This went on for years, until Thomas, now an adult, pushed back and removed himself from any meaningful relationship with his parents. He blamed them—and through them, the Christian church—for the pain and marginalization that he and the rest of the LGBTQ community felt. They had effectively locked themselves out of Thomas's life, which broke their hearts. They knew they were missing major milestones as Thomas excelled in his career, got involved in his community, became a homeowner, and fell in love with a guy named Trent, who became his partner. Thomas rarely called and was conspicuously absent at family gatherings and holidays.

The more Kevin and Beth shared with us, the more familiar their story felt. And so, Lynn and I did what seemed most natural: We shared our story in return. Over a series of dinner conversations, we talked about the seasons of fear and surviving our "new norm," and about the moments that had changed the way we understood our situation. God used some of the same moments that had meant so much to us to also reach them. When Beth heard the quote from Billy Graham about how it's God's job to judge and ours to love, it was as though lights flashed and bells rang in her head. God showed her that she was trying to control something that wasn't hers to own.

On another evening, when she brought up the challenge of supporting a son who "chose" to be gay, the door opened for Lynn and me to talk about what we'd learned from over a decade of relationships with LGBTQ people, both Christian and not. As we talked through the truth that not one person has ever told us "I *chose* this," we saw a new level of compassion growing in Beth's heart.

Lynn and I are careful never to tell another parent what they should do in their family relationship, but over time, we had the joy of watching Beth shift her perspective and embrace the idea of choosing love over judgment. We saw God convict her of her own mistakes and issues, and her heart was softened toward their son. And then the real work began.

Beth reached out to Thomas, who was understandably suspicious and hesitant of jumping back into a relationship. What took years to damage could not be restored overnight. But Beth was persistent. When Thomas gave her the cold shoulder, she kept reaching out. Finally, mother and son had a heart-wrenching confrontation. Beth spoke with candor about her own sin and mistakes, and Thomas started to believe that she'd changed. Slowly, the walls started to come down.

Lynn and I continued to meet with Kevin and Beth as they took tentative, sometimes awkward steps toward building a new relationship with Thomas. Over time, their relationship went from cold to vibrant. Thomas still has plenty of hesitation about the church and Christianity, but he no longer doubts his parents' love and concern for him.

Lynn

AS MUCH AS I loved sharing what God had done for me and Greg, we had limited experiences and definitely didn't (and still don't) have all the answers. Over and over, we sat down with parents and talked about tough issues. "How can I expect

my child to go to church when the people there say such painful things about him?" "I think his depression has turned into
substance abuse." "How do we explain to our younger kids
that their sister is a lesbian?" And so as Embracing the Journey
grew, it was also a privilege to step back and let other thriving
families share their perspective and experiences.

Parents who are navigating a transgender child's experiences, for example, have a lot of questions that Greg and I don't
have personal experience with. But we know many parents who
are further down that particular road, like a couple we'll call
Cindy and Norm. For many years, they'd struggled with the
idea that their daughter was gay, but that was nothing compared to the confusion that came when their child sat down
with them and explained that he was actually transgender. Over
time, and with a lot of love, prayer, and community support,
their fear turned to surviving, and then eventually thriving.
They eventually supported their child's transition and built a
new, stronger-than-ever relationship with their son. Today, the
family is crazy in love with each other, and each of their relationships with Jesus is deeper than ever. Cindy and Norm have
discovered the same passion that we did to help other families
learn from their mistakes and find hope in their story.

Greg and I started hosting dinners at our home specifically for parents of transgender children. Greg and I provide
the dinner and a safe space for Christian parents to share their
experiences, confusion, and questions, and then we step back
while people like Cindy and Norm share what they've learned.

This idea of creating a way for others to serve one another
has become an important part of our ministry, because when

you can take something that was once painful and see how God uses it to help others, another layer of healing happens.

Greg

THE MORE WE LISTENED to the hearts of others, the more people from all walks of life came alongside us and offered to help. Our vision for Embracing the Journey has always been to make it bigger than what Lynn and I do by ourselves, and now we have the platform and opportunity to include others and give them the opportunity to experience change as well. God has given us an incredible board, advisors, donors, and volunteers who come with their own stories, skill sets, and passions.

One of the coolest things that God has done through the launch of Embracing the Journey is to introduce us to smart, committed, and faithful people we'd never have met before, but who all have a passion for building bridges between churches, families, and the LGBTQ community.

Lynn

AS WE LOOK BACK, it's still amazing to me that God has given Greg and me the opportunity to bring together hurting people from across the country. Our story has been shared in front of groups bigger than the population of the town where we once lived. Sure, there are sacrifices. But the Lord has called us to this ministry, and life is good.

So far, our friend's concerns about what would happen if we "become the face of this" haven't come to pass. We do life with people who believe a lot of different things about the controversial topics of today, but we're not here to get involved in the culture wars. We're here to help people who are in the middle of a life they didn't expect move toward their family and move toward Jesus. We're here to talk about the Greatest Commandment, and how Jesus showed us time after time that we love him by loving each other well.

Greg

IN THE BEGINNING, ONE of the reasons Lynn and I committed to ministering to families was that we wanted to somehow redeem, or at least make up for, the things we did wrong in our own story. We talked a lot about not wanting people to make the same mistakes we did.

But today, I'm kind of beyond that. I feel like we repented, and Greg Jr. graciously forgave us, and that's become a piece of the past. Today, Lynn and I believe that God uniquely prepared us to be Greg Jr.'s parents, and realizing that made us see that our journey isn't about all the things we did wrong. It's the story of all the things God did right.

Like Joseph said to his brothers in Genesis, "You intended to harm me, but God intended it for good."

When we sat down to plan out this book, we spent a lot of time talking about its theme and purpose. It was Greg Jr. who nailed it. "This is a love story. It is a love story about a mom and dad pursuing their son while pursuing the Son of God."

As soon as he said it, we all instantly knew that he was right. Lynn's eyes welled up with tears of joy, as did mine. Our smart, creative, intuitive son, created in the image of God and placed in our lives to bring us to this place, saw through all the details of our story and found its heart.

Everything in our story comes back to love: the love of people for God, the love of parents for their son, the love of God for his creation, and the love of Christians for the church. This, we believe, is God's ultimate desire for us: to live in a daily love story that is directed by him and ultimately points to the love that he has for us.

Key Learnings: Make It Personal

+ Continue to invest yourself in deepening your understanding of your child's world. You probably won't be called to buy a condo in a historically gay neighborhood or start a full-time ministry, but you can read books or blogs written by others exploring the issues of faith and sexuality (there's a list of resources on our website to help parents, www.embracingthejourney.org), watch the movies or TV shows that your child relates to, and pay attention to current events that will specifically affect the LGBTQ community. Attend events that are designed to reconcile the Christian and LGBTQ communities, like Q Christian Fellowship conference. Let the community of people there help you to spark new conversations with your child about their own experience.

+ Look at your community in light of the Greatest Commandment to love your neighbor and ask whether
God is calling you to do something with this new experience in your family life. Your child has connected
you to a group of people who have been largely ne-
glected by the evangelical church. How can you, like
Jesus, shower them with mercy and grace? Here are
some things you can do to share God's love:

  + Host a Bible study in your home for a marginalized community that might not be comfortable
  in a traditional church setting.

  + Volunteer for an outreach program in your area
  that supports the LGBTQ community.

  + Approach your church and ask them to consider a Bible study or support group for parents
  of LGBTQ children.

  + Offer to be "surrogate" parents for someone
  who is LGBTQ and has a broken relationship
  with their own family. Invite them to holidays
  and family dinners. Call them to check in. Send
  them notes of encouragement.

+ If you still experience doubt or grief from time to time,
remind yourself that your child's sexuality is not some
cosmic accident. God created your child, and he created you to be exactly the parent that your child needs.

12

Let's Talk About Thriving

There was a time, not so long ago, when talking about all of this was hard.

We couldn't tell anyone that our son was gay without breaking into tears. We couldn't engage with him, or his friends, without feeling like we had to tell them why we thought they were wrong.

Life felt like one long struggle, and God felt terribly distant.

But then, little by little, things changed. The words that had once been devastating to us became the words that gave our lives joy, purpose, and meaning. The people who had once seemed so alien, so threatening to what we believed, became friends whom we loved dearly.

"How did you get from there to here?" asked a parent we met at a conference where we were sharing our story. Our answer was simple.

The Bible.

God gave us his word, recorded in Scripture and preserved for centuries, to show us the way he wanted us to live. The deeper we read his words, the more we understood that he doesn't want us to suffer in fear. He doesn't want us to persevere in misery. He wants us to *thrive*, full of the grace and love that comes only from a deep, trusting relationship with him.

Today, we are connected with parents, as well as many LGBTQ children, who are thriving in their relationships with God and with each other. They've embraced this journey that God has put in front of them, and through it they've found deeper, more meaningful ways to engage with him and love his creation.

What Do We Mean When We Talk About Thriving?

IN A WORLD THAT'S full of divisions and dissatisfaction, thriving is the willingness not just to accept, but also to celebrate the lives God gives us. It's an openness to let go of the dreams and expectations that defined us before and to see the beauty in a calling we never expected. It's never wanting to go back to the legalistic and judgmental way we were before we knew Greg Jr. was gay and celebrating instead the way God has reshaped and softened our hearts along the journey.

Thriving means experiencing each person we meet as a creation of God, made in his image as someone to be respected and not treated as a project. People who thrive accept that when Jesus said, "Love your neighbor as yourself," it wasn't a suggestion; it was a command. And they recognize that Jesus didn't exclude anyone—gay or straight, male or female, Christian or not—from who he sees as our neighbors.

We moved into the place we call thriving when we accepted that God chose us, people saved by grace and deeply in love with Jesus, to be Greg Jr.'s parents. He knew before our son was ever conceived how his life story would play out, and he trusted us to love Greg Jr. in the way he needed to be loved.

The practical details of thriving look different for everyone: Some parents with an LGBTQ child, like us, have embraced our connection to the community as an opportunity for ministry. We meet these families as they volunteer in programs that serve at-risk LGBTQ youth, as they lead the Parent Connect groups at our church, and as they sit at their computers for hours, praying for and encouraging people online. Thriving families join us in Embracing the Journey as volunteers and donors.

Other families thrive on a more intimate, personal scale. They find joy in one another. They let go of their agendas and formulas about what "the right" family looks like, and they embrace the beauty and complexity of the family they have. For them, thriving means enjoying the uniqueness of every person, offering them love with no strings attached, and discovering the joy of community as God intended, with no pressure on the outcome. There's no effort to change anyone, because only God can change a person's heart. Instead, thriving families support each member wherever they are and encourage one another to take one step closer to Jesus.

Families who are thriving are not perfect, of course. They still make mistakes with one another. The real difference is in their hearts. Their attention is not on the past or what *might have been*. Instead, they're focused on living in the present, in deep relationship with one another and with God. They understand that the world is dying to see people love one another, and they know the impact that their love has on those who are watching. What an incredible opportunity!

Thriving Doesn't Mean We Have All the Answers

EVER SINCE WE STARTED speaking publicly and writing about our experience, and especially since we've started to show Christians that they can thrive as parents of LGBTQ children, people have asked us to weigh in on big, controversial questions.

+ How do we respond to the verses in the Bible that address homosexuality?

+ What do we think about legalized gay marriage?

+ Why do we think that human beings are attracted to the same sex?

+ How do we respond to the latest quote from a famous pastor or media figure?

You've probably noticed that we don't tackle many hot topics like that in this book. That's not because we lack an opinion, but because we believe that God speaks to each person in his time. People don't thrive because they agree with what Greg and Lynn McDonald believe. They thrive because they are growing in their own faith, and that happens through their own experiences of pain, heartbreak, joy, and relationships. Then, through prayerful reading of Scripture and listening for God's whisper, they start to understand what *he* wants them to think about on any given topic, and how *he* wants them to act upon it.

To us, thriving isn't about being right. It's about being right with God.

At the end of the day, whether or not you agree with us on some hot topic doesn't matter. Whatever you believe, God calls us to love each other well.

There was a time, not so long ago, when the world seemed black and white to us. Everything had a definite answer of "right" or "wrong." People were either "good" or "bad." But the longer we live and the deeper we get with Jesus, the more we realize real life doesn't always work like that. Today we live in a Technicolor world.

We recently heard a pastor explain this idea in a way that finally released us from the idea that everything is either/or. He reminded us that in the beginning, Genesis says that "God called the light 'day,' and the darkness he called 'night.'" Yet we know that there is also dusk and dawn, gray periods between the two. Then God said, "Let the water under the sky be gathered to one place, and let dry ground appear," and "God called the dry ground land, and the gathered waters he called seas." The Bible doesn't talk about the streams, lakes, and rivers that dot the land, but that doesn't mean that those exist outside his will, or that the water there is somehow less important, or less biblical, than the oceans.

Some things are meant to be a mystery. Romans 11:33 says, "Oh, the depth of the riches of the wisdom and knowledge of God! How unsearchable his judgments, and his paths beyond tracing out!"

We've met many committed Christians who have studied, prayed, and sought God's guidance about issues related to the LGBTQ community, and they've come to some very different conclusions about some very big questions. We've listed a number of them for you in the resources list on our website, and if this is an issue close to your heart, we urge you to prayerfully dig deeper.

As for us, we're still praying, learning, and seeking God's truth. Every week, it seems, God shows us something new in Scripture about how we should live. The Holy Spirit convicts us when we need convicting and when we're open to his direction. He's changed our minds about some things and reassured us about others.

But in the end, our ability to thrive doesn't depend on how we translate a particular word in Paul's epistles or whether the gay couple at our dinner table is married or in a domestic partnership. Everything we believe comes down to this: *Love God, and love one another.* We leave the rest to the Holy Spirit.

What Does God Say About Thriving?

GOD'S DESIRE FOR US, his beloved creation, is that we thrive. "I have come that they may have life," said Jesus in John 10:10, "and have it to the full."

All of that suffering and perseverance that Paul talked about in Romans 5 was written so that we could get to this place of abundance. All those sleepless nights, tough conversations, and awkward moments existed so that we could reach this place of deep relationship with Jesus that he desires for us.

At the heart of thriving is this idea of love. "Dear friends, let us love one another, for love comes from God. Everyone who loves has been born of God and knows God" (1 John 4:7). A few verses later, God lays out the path to the fullness of life he desires for us: "Since God so loved us, we also ought to love one another. No one has ever seen God; but if we love one another, God lives in us and his love is made complete in us."

To be "complete" in God, then, is to love. That's why 1 Thessalonians tells us to "encourage one another and build each other up," and Jesus showed us time after time that we love him by loving each other well.

The path to thriving is not easy, or short. But the reward is eternal. Paul tells the Corinthians, "Do you not know that in a race all the runners run, but only one gets the prize? Run in such a way as to get the prize. Everyone who competes in the games goes into strict training. They do it to get a crown that will not last, but we do it to get a crown that will last forever" (1 Corinthians 9:24–25).

And again, in Colossians: "Whatever you do, work heartily, as for the Lord and not for men, knowing that from the Lord you will receive the inheritance as your reward. You are serving the Lord Christ."

What Does It Take to Live a Life of Thriving?

EVERY PERSON WHOSE LIFE has been thrown off track by an obstacle or surprise longs for the reassurance that they will once again return to the way it once was, but in reality, it's hard to go back to the past. The good news is that God never wastes anything.

We have found that the key to thriving is to find the greater purpose behind the pain. The mountaintop experiences are fun and exhilarating, but things grow best in the fertile soil of the valley below.

If you have gone through a radical life change, the valley you have passed through hopefully will deepen your relationship with God, equipping you for a life you wouldn't have otherwise been prepared for. For us, our new lives of thriving meant losing a lot of our old ideas about religion and becoming better followers of Jesus. The way we experience church, and the people we encounter every day, will never be the same again.

It begins, as we've seen, with being honest. You can't thrive if you're constantly pretending to be what you think you're supposed to be or worrying about being judged. Letting go of your pride means letting go of the idea that you're somehow better than someone else.

Our journey toward thriving began the moment when God whispered, "Let's talk about your sin." Whenever we're tempted to feel superior, or to think we're doing better than someone else, those words come back. Yes, as Christians we are "new creations in Christ Jesus," but we are also sinners, and yet God loves us.

When you're honest about your story, and open with the things that are happening in your life, you invite deeper authenticity from others. When you act in love, without hidden motives or ultimatums, you will find a closer connection to Jesus, the ultimate example of love.

From there, have courage to read the Bible. Ask God to give you fresh eyes to see his truth through the lenses of his greatest commandments to love. Read commentaries from a variety of perspectives that offer insights to the authors of specific books within the Bible, the audiences to whom they were writing, and how those messages applied in the culture in which they were written. God will show you what you need to learn.

Thriving requires a willingness to let go, acknowledging that God doesn't need you to fix what seems broken. We thrive when we trust that God has a plan, and that his desire for us is better than anything we can do ourselves.

Yes, some people will disappoint you. Some people will reject your efforts to love. Some will choose judgment. But you'll be surprised how many people will show up for you, and those relationships you form will be authentic. They will produce sure footing when you are in need, and they'll give you the opportunity to provide safety for others when they need you.

God designed humans to love one another: our friends, our church, and yes, even those who seem like our enemies.

It's not always easy, but we're made to live together in fellowship—to help one another, to bear one another's burdens, and to encourage those around us to keep going. There is something life-giving about taking the focus off ourselves and helping others.

"And let us consider how we may spur one another on toward love and good deeds, not giving up meeting together, as some are in the habit of doing, but encouraging one another—and all the more as you see the Day approaching" (Hebrews 10:24–25).

Our unexpected journey has brought us to a place where we can be grateful for the opportunity to offer hope to the hopeless, help others embrace their journey, and experience true peace and contentment.

When we finally let go of our own desires, fears, ambitions, and pride, and we put ourselves out there as flawed creations who sought only to love, God rewarded us with a sense of belonging, joy, and grace that we'd never experienced before. He allowed us to thrive.

Afterword

Fast-forward to today.

As we write this, we are almost twenty years into our journey as the parents of a gay son, and we're grateful to report that our family is closer than ever.

In 2017, we sold the condo in Boystown. We hadn't been able to visit as often now that we lived farther away, and Greg Jr. was ready to try something new. He moved to Atlanta, and for the first time since they became adults, both of our kids now live just a short drive from us, and from each other. It's such a blessing to be part of their everyday lives.

We wish every family could have the kind of close, honest relationship that we have today. Our son—the same person who once said it felt like he didn't have parents—is now an important part of our ministry. Greg Jr. travels with us to conferences, edits our blog posts, and keeps us informed about changes in culture and language.

The world is dramatically different than it was in the summer of 2001 when Greg Jr. came out, especially when it comes to how the LGBTQ community is accepted and treated. The AIDS crisis and the painful rumors that swirled around us back then seem like a distant memory. Being gay is no longer something that people, especially young people, feel like they need to hide. Marriage is legal. Society as a whole is better at talking about homosexuality and is now tackling other issues, like transgender identity.

As parents, we celebrate that our son doesn't have to live in the shadows. But as Christians, our hearts still ache to see that the culture shifts have left our beloved Christian community divided.

Unlike the early days when we couldn't find a single book or resource to guide us, bookstores today carry a collection of personal narratives and Bible studies from gay Christian writers, while events and social media connect thousands of LGBTQ Christians and broadcast their stories. In the last decade, many evangelical pastors and leaders have publicly supported including the LGBTQ community in their churches and making every person feel welcome in God's kingdom. Others have doubled down on those six verses in Scripture that seem to condemn homosexuality, going so far as to say that Christians who support the LGBTQ community are heretics outside God's kingdom.

We're friends with people on both sides of the debate and with plenty who are somewhere in the middle. We know that they all love Jesus and love the Bible. But when churches start talking about the LGBTQ community, all too often denominations split. Pastors leave, or church members do.

As followers of Christ, we still have a long way to go to find unity, and thousands of families are caught in the middle.

A Pew Research study says that one in five American adults would be "very upset" if their child came out as gay or lesbian,* and almost 40 percent of LGBTQ adults say that they were rejected by a family member or close friend because of their sexual orientation or gender identity.†

According to the best estimates from the National Alliance to End Homelessness, almost half of the 1.3 million to 1.7 million American youth who are homeless at least one night of the year are LGBTQ. We've met many of them right here in Atlanta, where we volunteer with a nonprofit called Lost-n-Found Youth, a homeless shelter specifically for LGBTQ youth. The overwhelming reason for their homelessness is family rejection.

Those numbers break our hearts and remind us of our calling. We know how easy it is to react in fear when faced with a reality that shakes our foundational values. We know how much parents love their kids and want what's best for them, and also how easy it is to say and do hurtful, relationship-breaking things in the heat of a moment. We've been there.

But the people we meet face-to-face give us hope that every day new bridges are being built between the LGBTQ community, their families, and the church, so let's end our time together with a story.

While we were working on this book, we got a phone call from a woman in another state. Jackie found our website and

---

*Bruce Drake, "How LGBT Adults See Society and How the Public Sees Them," Pew Research Center, June 25, 2013, http://www.pewresearch.org/fact-tank/2013/06/25/how-lgbt-adults-see-society-and-how-the-public-sees-them/.

†Pew Research Center's Social & Demographic Trends Project, "A Survey of LGBT Americans," June 13, 2013, http://www.pewsocialtrends.org/2013/06/13/a-survey-of-lgbt-americans/.

was desperate enough to reach out to us, complete strangers. Her son is gay, and her husband, Bob, was mired deep in the place of fear. He wouldn't acknowledge their child. He wouldn't talk to his wife about what was happening. For four years, they'd been keeping their family's reality a secret from everyone. They hadn't told a single person: not a friend, not a family member, not a pastor.

The secrecy and shame were eating Jackie alive, and she started asking God to bring someone into their lives who she and her husband could talk to. She started randomly googling, and God led her to Embracing the Journey. When she saw our video testimony, she felt like we were safe.

She asked if we would meet on the phone, which we were happy to do. But as we listened to the pain in this woman's voice, we offered something else.

"If you ever want to come to Atlanta, we'd love to meet with you in person. It's a great city to visit, and we'll clear our schedule and have a chance to really talk."

It's a sign of how much this couple was hurting that they agreed. Jackie and Bob set aside a weekend and flew to Georgia, and the four of us spent hours together, deeply sharing our experiences. We didn't show up with a formula or a formal program. We just listened, and asked questions, and prayed together. We reassured them that they weren't alone and that there was a path from the place of fear to the place where their family can once again thrive. Most of all, we offered love without judgment—for them, for their child, and for their church community.

We assured them, in words and by example, that while

what they were feeling now was real, life could look different someday. There was hope.

As Jackie and Bob opened up, we could see a visible change in their demeanors. The weight that had been on their shoulders for so long started to lighten. Their family was no longer a secret. They went home to face the next step on their journey with God.

And we stayed in Atlanta, close to the children God gave us to love, knowing that the phone would soon ring again.

Study Guide

Part 1: Fear (Chapters 1–4)

1. The first thing Greg and Lynn did when they found evidence that Greg Jr. was gay was to make an appointment with their pastor and seek his advice on what "a Christlike response" to their situation would be. If you were their pastor, how would you answer their question? How do you think Jesus would respond to a gay teenager?

2. When Lynn and Greg found out that their son was gay, they were shocked that he had been keeping it a secret from them. But when they stepped back and considered the environment they'd created, and the messages they'd given their children about "those people," they had to reconsider. What messages do you communicate to the people closest to you, including your children, about sexuality and gender?

3. Greg and Lynn developed many of their negative impressions and ideas about homosexuality and "the gay agenda" from Christian media figures that they trusted. Where did your ideas about sexuality and gender come from? Think

about the earliest messages you heard about homosexuality. How do those messages affect your perspective today?

4. Greg says that "We felt like we had a great relationship with our kids, and to find out that one of them was hiding something this big was a huge betrayal." But the more they thought about it, the more the McDonalds realized they hadn't created a safe environment for their son to talk about his sexual identity. If someone close to you (a child, family member, or close friend) was gay, do you think that you would be a safe person for them to share their experiences with? Why or why not?

5. Have you ever been in a position where you wanted to tell someone something personal or troubling, but felt like they were not a safe person to trust with your secret? How did that situation work out?

6. After they realized that their son was gay, Greg became more aware of how often those around him made jokes or derogatory comments about gay people, and how often he'd participated. How do you respond when someone makes jokes or disrespectful comments about gay people or other minority groups? Why do you respond the way you do?

7. Has someone ever tried to "fix" something about the way you acted, believed, or lived? How did their actions make you feel at the time?

8. Lynn's perspective changes radically when God speaks to her and says, "Today, let's talk about your sin." She's reminded of Jesus' words: "Why do you look at the speck of sawdust in your brother's eye and pay no attention to the plank in your own eye? . . . You hypocrite, first take the plank out of your own eye." Is there a "plank" in your eye right now that Jesus is challenging you to deal with? What does God want you to deal with in your own heart today?

9. Have you experienced a season of fear—the kind that "shreds our ability to think with a dump-truck load of worst-case scenario images"—that Greg and Lynn described in this section? What caused it? Looking back, was it a rational fear or an irrational fear?

10. Lynn and Greg say that "getting past our fear begins with getting out of the dark closet and getting honest with God and ourselves." 1 Peter says that we can "leave all your worries with him, because he cares for you." Have you experienced a time in your life when you surrendered something to God and found release from fear and worry? Are you currently holding on to a fear that is weighing you down? What do you need to do to turn it over to God?

Part 2: Surviving (Chapters 5–8)

1. Greg quotes Martin Luther King Jr., who said, "In the end, we will remember not the words of our enemies, but the silence of our friends." Have you ever been in a situation where

you were silent while a friend went through a difficult time? What held you back from acting? What could you have done differently?

2. Although Greg was personally uncomfortable that his son was gay, his anger flared when a family member criticized Greg Jr., and then again when anonymous people in his town wrote hateful messages on the sidewalk. How do you respond when someone criticizes a person you love? Does your response change if the criticism is related to something that makes you uncomfortable?

3. Certain stories from the Bible speak to us and affect how we understand our calling as Christians. For Lynn and Greg, it was Jesus' parable about the Good Samaritan, and then later his encounter with the woman caught in adultery. What is your favorite story of Jesus? Go back and read it again, even if it feels familiar to you. What does it show you about how Jesus loved?

4. Greg and Lynn's pastor encouraged them to not only love their son, but to love his friends. This became a testing ground for them, as they interacted for the first time with people who were openly LGBTQ. Are there people in your life now who it's easy to show love to? Are there types of people who are more difficult for you to love? Why?

5. What is your reaction to the familiar phrase "Love the sinner, hate the sin"? Is there a biblical basis for the idea? How

have you seen Christians try to live out this idea, and how did that work out?

6. James 4:12 says, "There is only one Lawgiver and Judge, the one who is able to save and destroy. But you—who are you to judge your neighbor?" This is one of the foundations of the Billy Graham quote: "It is the Holy Spirit's job to convict, God's job to judge, and my job to love." How are these three things—convicting, judging, and loving—different? Are there places in your life where you are stepping into a job not meant for you?

7. Even as Lynn and Greg rebuilt a relationship with their openly gay son, one of the hardest things to accept was the thought of him in a relationship with another man. How do you feel about interacting and developing friendships with same-sex couples? Where do those feelings come from?

8. After a long, confusing, exhausting period where they tried to change their son and his friends, Greg and Lynn turned to the Bible with a specific question: "How did Jesus treat those who lived differently than he did?" How would you answer this question? When you look at Jesus' life, what stands out to you about the way he interacted with other people?

9. Lynn acknowledges that many of the mistakes she and Greg made during this season of surviving came from their pride and their concern about their reputations. "Being seen as good Christians was more important to us than how we treated each

other. Our reputation was more important than our family." Why do you think people care so much about how others see them?

10. Many of the mistakes and misdirection that Greg and Lynn experienced in this season came from a desire to try to control their situation. Although they didn't realize it at the time, they'd started to believe Satan's lie that God needed help to handle the difficult corners of their lives. Is there a relationship in your life that you're struggling to control? What would it mean to surrender it to God?

11. In our society today, perseverance and endurance are traits that are often admired and encouraged. Yet Greg and Lynn make a case here that God wants more for us than that. Is there a place in your life where you feel like you're merely surviving, trying to get from day to day? What would it take for you to move into a place of hope and abundance?

Part 3: Thriving (Chapters 9–12)
1. Greg and Lynn started their journey believing that the Bible was clear about how to act toward people who were gay. But the more they read, the more the Bible surprised them. They conclude that "our path toward a ministry of reconciliation happened not in spite of the Bible, but because of it." Has there been a time when the Bible surprised you? What did you learn? How did it change the way you interact with others?

2. After Jesus explained the two greatest commandments—to love God and to love our neighbors—he said, "All the Law and the Prophets hang on these two commandments." What do you think he meant by that? Does this sentence change the way you view other instructions or guidelines in the Bible?

3. Greg and Lynn pushed themselves way outside their comfort zones when they bought a condo in Boystown, a historically LGBTQ neighborhood. Have you ever lived in a neighborhood where you were a cultural minority? What did it teach you?

4. The LGBTQ people Lynn and Greg met in Chicago told them about their previous experiences with Christians, including those who waved signs that said they were going to hell. How would you respond to someone who had experienced that? What do you think a Christlike response would be to a pride parade?

5. Cancer was a "game changer" for the entire McDonald family. Has there been some unexpected event in your life that changed your perspective on life? How did it affect your faith?

6. Lynn wasn't sure at first that she was willing to go public with her experience as the Christian mother of a gay son, because she felt like she would get "battered from both sides." Greg, on the other hand, looked at "being the face of this" and said, "Bring it on." If you were in their position, how would you react? Would you share your opinion on a controversial

topic if you thought that people you respect would disagree or get offended?

7. When Greg and Lynn moved to Atlanta, they looked for a church home that was both biblically grounded and balanced in both truth and grace. What do those descriptions mean to you? What do you think a "balanced" church looks like, especially as it relates to the LGBTQ community?

8. God wants us to live full and abundant lives. What does that mean for you? What would an abundant life look like?

9. What do you think Paul meant in Romans 11:33 when he wrote that God's judgments are "unsearchable . . . and his paths beyond tracing out"? Do you see certain things in God's creation as "gray" or mysterious, beyond our limited definitions of "right" and "wrong"? How does that change the way you act?

10. As you finish this book, has anything changed about the way you think about or how you feel about God, the LGBTQ community, or the responsibility of Christ followers?

Resource Guide

When we started our journey as the parents of a gay son, we couldn't find a single book, article, or story to help us. Today, things have changed. On our website, we've compiled and continue to update a Resource page with links to books, articles, videos, and websites that helped us on our journey and that might help you on yours.

Check it out at www.embracingthejourney.org/Resources.